P9-CRN-680

MAYORS OF TORONTO

Volume 1
1834-1899

MAYORS OF TORONTO

Volume 1
1834–1899

VICTOR LORING RUSSELL

Victor L. Russell
Sept 1982

THE BOSTON MILLS PRESS

THE ONTARIO HISTORICAL SOCIETY

ISBN 0-919822-77-0

Copyright © Victor Russell, 1982

Front Cover:
  William Lyon Mackenzie, Mayor of Toronto, 1834 (oil on
  canvas) Portrait by J.W.L. Forster (1900); Collection of the
  Corporation of the City of Toronto.

Back Cover:
  John Shaw, Mayor of Toronto, 1899 (oil on canvas) Portrait by
  J.W.L. Forster (n.d.); Collection of the Corporation of the City
  of Toronto.

PHOTO CREDITS
  Public Archives of Canada: p. 12; p. 65.
  Metropolitan Toronto Library: p. 103; p. 107.
  All other visuals courtesy of The City of Toronto Archives.

Published in Canada by
THE BOSTON MILLS PRESS
  98 Main Street
  Erin, Ontario NOB ITO

We gratefully acknowledge the assistance of the Canada
Council and the Ontario Arts Council in the publishing of this
book.

The Canada Council
Conseil des Arts du Canada
1957-1982

Winners of the
Heritage Canada
Communications Award

CONTENTS
MAYORS OF TORONTO   1834-1899

For ADAM and ANNE

FOREWORD

The publication of this volume marks the end of the first part of a project I have envisioned for a number of years. It began in 1974 when I was hired by Mr. A. R. N. Woadden, the City Archivist and now Deputy City Clerk, to compile biographical files on all of the men who had served as Mayor of Toronto. During the next few years, as these files were added to, it became evident that a small volume of biographical sketches of the Mayors would be a useful reference tool for anyone interested in the history of the City. It goes without saying that virtually each individual would make an interesting study in his own right. However, the intent of this volume is to re-introduce the men who have served as Mayor of our City, from 1834 to 1899, in brief staightforward biographies.

I believe it is fair to say that the basic duties involved in holding the position of Mayor of Toronto has changed little over time; simply, the Mayor was the chief executive officer of the Corporation and as such chaired City Council, was ex-officio member of all committees and was expected to perform all ceremonial duties related to the Corporation. What has changed, however, is the City. William Lyon MacKenzie was Mayor of an isolated colonial outpost with a population of less than 10,000, whose streets were unpaved, whose buildings were predominantly wooden and that was, for all intents and purposes, void of municipal services. On the other hand, by 1899, John Shaw was

7

presiding over a City Council that represented a population of 193,246, boasted of many services such as a full scale professional police force of some 300 men and nearly 200 miles of sewers; in all the City Council for 1899 administered an annual budget of more than $8,000,000.00. Rather than a comprehensive chronicle of this development, this work endeavours to begin to explore the individual contributions of the men who occupied the Mayor's chair for the first 65 years of its history.

For the purposes of information as well as clarity, a brief note should be made about the method of electing the Mayor. On 6 March 1834 the government of Upper Canada passed a bill entitled 'An Act to extend the limits of the Town of York, to erect the said Town into a City, and to incorporate it under the name of the City of Toronto." Three weeks later, on 27 March, the inhabitants of the new city voted in their first civic election, returning two Aldermen and two Councilmen from each of the five designated wards.

The first task of the newly elected City Council was to choose, from among the Aldermen-elect, the first Mayor of the City. To that end the council was ceremoniously convened at 12 o'clock noon on Thursday, April 3rd 1834 at the Town Hall in the St Lawrence Market. Mr John Doel, a brewer and Councilman-elect for St Andrew's Ward, was asked to the chair; he then called for nominations and accordingly Mr Franklin Jackes, seconded by Mr Lesslie, moved that Alderman-elect for St David's Ward, "William Lyon MacKenzie be Mayor of this City." After some heated debate the question was carried by a vote of 10 to 8, and the Mayor took his place at the dais to return thanks for "the honour that had been conferred upon him."

Although there were minor variations involving the election of Aldermen and Councilmen in the years that followed, the same procedure for electing the Mayor was followed until 1858; the council would assemble after the annual municipal elections in January of each year to elect from amongst the Aldermen, their presiding officer. The first popular elections for the Mayoralty took place in 1858 with the election of Sir Adam Wilson. Public election of the Mayor continued until 1867, when, once again, the Mayor was to be chosen by City Council from among its members. Council at this time was composed of three Aldermen from each Ward, the position of Councilman had been discontinued by the Municipal

Institutions Act of 1866. Election of the Mayor by the public, or popular vote, was re-introduced in 1874 and has remained the responsibility of the ratepayers of the City to this day.

Acknowledgements

As is customary, I would like to extend my appreciation to people around me who supported the project over the years: R. Scott James, City Archivist of Toronto, for his constant support; Charles Dougall, Editor at the *Dictionary of Canadian Biography* for his helpful suggestions on the first drafts; and Paul Romney for his patient review of the manuscript. Thanks are due to Glenda Wilson for expertly typing the manuscript and to Linda Price for her help with organizing and selecting the visuals.

Victor L. Russell

1834-1844
Following the Incorporation of the City of Toronto in March 1834, City Council met in the gallery of this building on King Street near Jarvis. Built in 1831 as a Market and Town Hall, this quadrangular brick structure was the seat of municipal government until 1844. It was destroyed in the Great Fire of 1849 which destroyed many other buildings in the area and was replaced by the St. Lawrence Hall.

1845-1899
Constructed in 1844 from competition-winning designs of architect Henry Bower Lane, this Georgian style building located at Front and Jarvis Streets served as City Hall until 1899. The centre portion of the building, which housed the Council Chamber, exists today as a part of the south St. Lawrence Market building, and is occupied by the City of Toronto Archives Market Gallery.

1899-1945
Known today as "Old" City Hall, this beautiful Romanesque structure was designed by architect Edward James Lennox. Begun in 1889, construction was not completed for nearly 10 years. It was officially opened on 18 September 1899 by Mayor John Shaw.

WILLIAM LYON MACKENZIE, journalist and politician; b. 12 March 1795 at Springfield, Dundee, Scotland, the only son of Daniel and Elizabeth Chalmers Mackenzie (*née* Mackenzie); grandfather of William Lyon Mackenzie King, Prime Minister of Canada; d. 28 August 1861 in Toronto.

WILLIAM LYON MACKENZIE
MAYOR 1834

William Lyon Mackenzie arrived in Upper Canada from Scotland in April 1820, and after a few years in business at Dundas he moved to Queenston. On 18 May 1824 he launched his career in political journalism by publishing the first issue of the *Colonial Advocate.* Mackenzie, through his newspaper, was soon a leading voice of the growing reform movement and to be closer to the provincial parliament moved his operation to York in the fall of 1824.

Mackenzie's forthright and forceful manner, together with his ardent denunciation of the "Family Compact," contributed much to his popularity, and in 1828 he was easily elected to the House of Assembly for the riding of York. However, Mackenzie's venomous attacks on the local oligarchy also caused reprisals. In the few years preceding his election as Mayor, Mackenzie's political views and "Firebrand" demands for reform, produced libel suits, threats and physical assaults, as well as an attack on his newspaper establishment which left the office wrecked and the type thrown into the lake. The diminutive Scot's scathing attacks on the "Compact" also led to his repeated expulsion from the assembly, although he was consistently returned by his constituents. In the midst of all this, it is easy to understand why his reform colleagues, who had won a majority on the newly created municipal council in 1834, elected him Mayor.

Mackenzie approached the mayoralty with characteristic enthusiasm and energy. Leading a bitterly divided council through its formative days, the new Mayor faced difficult questions such as contested elections (in four of the five wards), and the appointment of important civic officials — City Clerk, City Chamberlain, and Clerk of the Market. The Mayor also had important judicial duties to perform: as chief Magistrate he was expected to attend to the police office every day to deal with petty cases, and to preside over the Mayor's Court at least one week every three months to deal with more serious offenders. It was proposed that the Mayor receive £250 for all these administrative and judicial duties but, true to his beliefs, Mackenzie had the salary reduced to the statutory minimum of £100. Moreover, his sense of duty went beyond prescribed tasks: during the ravages of a cholera epidemic in the summer of 1834, which killed more than 500 of the City's 10,000 inhabitants, Mackenzie worked tirelessly until he too was ill. It is appropriate that during MacKenzie's mayoralty the city council adopted a design for a coat of arms and a civic motto (reported by some to have been suggested by the Mayor) of "Industry, Intelligence, Integrity."

At the end of 1834, Mackenzie made it clear that he would not serve a second term. He had been elected to the provincial parliament again in the fall of 1834 and had decided it was more important to pursue the cause of reform in the provincial arena. However, frustration followed disappointment, and in December 1837 an embittered Mackenzie organized and led an obortive armed revolt. With the collapse of the rebellion, he escaped to the United States, where he continued to work for the "Liberation of Upper Canadians" until he was jailed by American authorities for breach of the neutrality laws. After 18 months in jail, he spent the next 10 years in exile in the United States, eventually finding suitable employment as a correspondent for the *New York Tribune*. During his exile, he completed several books, including *The Sons of the Emerald Isle* (1844),*The Lives and Opinions of Benjamin Franklin Butler and Jessee Hayt* (1845), and *The Life and Times of Martin Van Buren* (1846).

William Lyon Mackenzie gladly returned to Canada in 1849 following a pardon from the government. Undaunted and somewhat unrepentant, he quickly resumed both his journalistic and his political careers, serving with characteristic energy in the assembly of the Province of Canada for Haldimand until retirement in 1857, and publishing from time to time a political squib usually entitled *Mackenzie's Weekly Message*. Toronto's first Mayor, the fiery and principled Scotsman, died at home on Bond Street in Toronto on August 28th, 1861.

ROBERT BALDWIN SULLIVAN, politician, lawyer and judge; b. 24 May 1802 at Bandon, near Cork, Ireland, the second son of Daniel and Barbara Sullivan (*née* Baldwin); m. first in 1829 Cecelia Eliza Matthews, daughter of Captain John Matthews, and secondly in 1833 Emily Louisa Delatre; d. 14 April 1853 in Toronto.

ROBERT BALDWIN SULLIVAN
MAYOR 1835

Robert Baldwin Sullivan was the second Mayor of Toronto. In the 1835 civic elections he led the aldermanic poll in St David's Ward, defeating Willim Lyon Mackenzie (q.v.) who had, however, indicated that he could not serve a second term. When the city council-elect met on January 15th, 1835 to choose a Mayor, Sullivan, a young but erudite lawyer, was the unanimous choice.

Born and educated in Ireland, Sullivan came to Upper Canada with his family in 1819. His father, a merchant in Ireland, established a business in York, apparently to be near his well-known relatives, the Baldwins. Young Sullivan was placed on the books of the Law Society of Upper Canada in 1823 and articled to his famous uncle Dr William Warren Baldwin. During his five years as a law student Sullivan served as librarian to the House of Assembly, a position he no doubt owed to his uncle's influence. Called to the bar in 1828, he was soon involved in politics, travelling to Vittoria, Norfolk County, to conduct Dr Baldwin's election campaign for the House of Assembly. Afterwards, he remained in Vittoria where he married the daughter of leading local reformer, Captain John Matthews, and set up a law office. Sullivan's subsequent involvement in several notorious and politically controversial legal actions, most notably the libel trial of Francis Collins and the contested election hearings involving Dr Thomas David Morrison (q.v.) and John Beverley Robinson, established his reputation as an extremely

17

talented lawyer. Indeed, it has been suggested that he possessed one of the most brilliant legal minds of his day. In any case, following the death of his wife in 1830, he returned to York to practise law first with his uncle, and then with the latter's son, his cousin and brother-in-law, Robert Baldwin.

As Mayor, Sullivan added much to the dignity of the proceedings of the city council by creating a businesslike atmosphere, which was amplified by the addition of official "robes of office" for the Mayor. His absence on one occasion, in fact, led to a complete breakdown of decorum when Alderman George Duggan, elected to the chair *pro tempore*, refused to entertain a motion duly seconded. This created such a ruckus that Duggan was forced to leave the council chamber. He was later found guilty of contempt and high breach of the privileges of the council and forced to make a suitable apology. Generally, however, the council under Sullivan's leadership considered more serious municipal matters such as tax rates, grants to Hook & Ladder Company, and the removal of the filth and nuisances from the city's streets. Undoubtedly the most important achievment of the 1835 Council was the decision to build Toronto's first sewer. On May 6th, 1835 the committee on draining and paving recommended, at a cost of £4,125, the construction of a main sewer on King Street into which all subsequent drains and sewers could be connected.

Sullivan's election as alderman and Mayor in 1835 was his first and only attempt at elective office. He did, however, continue his rise to prominence, and played an important role in the political life of the province. Appointed to the executive council as its president by Lieutenant-Governor Sir Francis Bond Head in 1836, Sullivan also became Commissioner of Crown Lands, a position he held until 1841. In February 1839 he was appointed to the legislative council, and as such he played a leading role in the support of Governor Charles Poulett Thompson (Lord Sydenham) as well as the accomplishment of the union of the Canadas in 1841. He was appointed to the legislative council again in that year and acted as first president of the executive council of the united province.

Sullivan resigned from the government later that year in support of the demands of the Baldwin-Lafontaine ministry. This incident led to a public dispute between Sullivan and Egerton Ryerson over the principles of responsible government. Sullivan, using the nom de plume LEGION, devastated Ryerson in an exchange of letters in the newspapers, demonstrating without question his talent for conducting logical and rational argument. Sullivan was to return to the executive council in the second Baldwin-Lafontaine ministry, only to resign when elevated to the bench, serving as puisne judge of the court of Queen's Bench until 1850 when he acted in the Court of Common Pleas.

Sullivan, without question one of the most talented men ever to be Mayor, was at times disdainful of politics, and although his private life was upset with bouts of alcoholism, his public life was characterized by appointments from all parties, who quite wisely attempted to make use of his considerable intellectual ability.

THOMAS DAVID MORRISON, physician and politician; b. about 1796 at Quebec City; d. 19 March 1856 at Toronto.

THOMAS DAVID MORRISON
MAYOR 1836

The third Mayor, Dr Thomas David Morrison, was a well known physician and a long-time resident of Toronto. Some time before 1816 he had come to the town of York where he was employed as a clerk in the surveyor general's office. Dismissed apparently for participating in the organization of the first Methodist church in Toronto in 1818, Morrison had been a member of the Church of England (a "nominal churchman"), and his conversion to Methodism was looked upon as a serious deviation from the values held by the provincial "officialdom" centred at "little York." Following his dismissal he travelled to the United States, probably Michigan, to study medicine. He returned to York a few years later, and after being examined by the Upper Canada Medical Board on July 5th, 1824 was licensed as a physician. He soon established a large practice in the town as well as "in the country up Yonge Street."

Partly perhaps as a result of his unfortunate earlier dealings with the "official party," Morrison was a supporter of the reform movement in Upper Canada. He entered the provincial election of 1828, which was held during the excitement caused by the dismissal of Judge John Walpole Willis, who had questioned the practices of the legal establishment. Morrison's opponent on the hustings was none other than that pillar of the establishment, John Beverley Robinson. The ensuing contest which Morrison lost by 17 votes,

21

was a heated one. The result was disputed, and the hearings themselves became a *cause célèbre*. Nevertheless, Robinson's election was upheld. Morrison eventually won election to the assembly in 1834, serving as a member for Toronto until 1837.

Prior to his election as Mayor in 1836, Morrison had been involved in numerous community activities. In 1831 he served as vice-president of the Bible Society of York, for many years was a trustee of the Toronto General Burying Grounds. In 1832 he joined his friends and colleagues Drs W.W. Baldwin and John E. Tims in announcing the establishment of the York Dispensary. Opened on August 22nd, 1832, the dispensary lasted about one year, during which it prescribed and distributed free medicine to 746 patients at a cost of £118.3s.4d. Morrison, like most 19th-century doctors, spent much of his time courageously fighting the cholera epidemics that ravaged urban centres. To this end, he served on the various local boards of health and in 1836 served as president of the Toronto Board of Health.

Although during Morrison's mayoralty, the reform dominated city council did spend much of its time considering municipal improvements, such as the problems inherent in a water works system and "lighting the streets with gas," like previous councils it was very much caught up with the provincial political scene. In February 1836 Morrison as Mayor signed an optimistic welcome address to the new lieutenant-governor, Sir Francis Bond Head, who reformers on council and throughout the province hoped would help them secure the desired reforms. It was soon appparent, however, that their optimism was misplaced, and by the end of 1836 the council passed a motion of non-confidence in the provincial administration. As the agitation for reform intensified in 1837, Morrison played a central role. He attended meetings such as the famous one called at John Doel's brewery in November 1837, but demurred at signing a plan for revolt. Although he subsequently played no part in the rebellion of December 1837, he was arrested and tried for high treason. Defended by Robert Baldwin, he was acquitted but, fearing further persecution, he fled to the United States.

Dr Morrison remained in exile for 5 years settling in Batavia, New York, where he established himself in practice. In 1843, following a declaration of amnesty which included all Upper

Canadian rebels except William Lyon Mackenzie (q.v.), he returned to Toronto and re-established his practice there. Unlike Mackenzie, however, he did not seek public office. Instead he concentrated on his medical career, serving on various hospital boards and lecturing at the Toronto School of Medicine.

Dr Thomas David Morrison's political career was inextricably connected with the fortunes of the provincial reform movement which was soundly defeated in December 1837. This is especially true of his term as Mayor, when he presided over a council preoccupied with provincial concerns. Dr Morrison died quietly at his home on Adelaide Street on March 19th, 1856.

GEORGE GURNETT, journalist, politician, and Police Magistrate; b. about 1791 in Sussex, England; d. 17 November 1861 in Toronto.

GEORGE GURNETT
MAYOR 1837, 1848-50

Perhaps the man most devotedly involved in the early development of municipal government in Toronto was the fourth Mayor, George Gurnett. He sat as councilman for St George's Ward on the first council, in 1834, and after that as alderman for the same ward until 1851. From the beginning he served, usually as chairman, on the important committees of council, such as finance and assessment and the board of works. Indeed, Gurnett's domination of civic affairs was so pronounced that by 1841 the usually calm and moderate Robert Baldwin remarked that Toronto has become "a rotten borough under the control of an ignorant and violent faction," a faction led, he said, by Gurnett.

Gurnett was born about 1792 in Sussex, England. Little is known of his early life other than that he came to North America while in his late 20's, settling first in Virginia. Soon afterwards, probably in 1826, he moved to Ancaster, Upper Canada, where he pursued a career in journalism. The first edition of his local paper, *The Gore Gazette*, appeared on March 3rd, 1827, and soon became a leading propagandist on behalf of the local establishment, or "Family Compact." The future Mayor was personally involved in the tarring and feathering of a local reform politician in 1828; in 1829 he vigorously supported Allan Napier McNab's contemptible behaviour during and following the notorious Tory riot, dubbed the

"Hamilton Outrage," during which the Lieutenant Governor was burned in effigy.

In 1829 Gurnett moved his printing operation to York and renamed his paper, *The Courier of Upper Canada*. His vociferous support of the "government men" brought him much public support and attention, but, at the same time, it brought him into direct, and often personal, opposition to William Lyon Mackenzie (q.v.). Gurnett seldom passed over a chance to assail his opponent and he received the same treatment from his equally abrasive enemy. His attacks on the members of the reform movement were often devastating, but they also often embarrassed those he supported.

During his 17 years on city council, Gurnett was Mayor four times: in 1837, 1848, 1849 and 1850. During his first mayoralty, he was appointed a magistrate of the Home District and district clerk of the peace. Wearing these many caps, and consistent with his political affiliations, he took a leading role in the organization of the defences of the city during the Rebellion, though others, most notably John Powell (q.v.) received the praise. When he became Mayor again in 1848 it was his administrative skills and knowledge of civic government rather than his political bias that won him the job. Unfortunately, he was Mayor during another disaster — the first great fire, which destroyed the centre of the business district and St James Cathedral. His three successive terms (1848-50) were not, however, overwhelmed by disaster. He took an active lead in promoting Toronto as a burgeoning metropolitan centre. In 1850, for example, he presided over a public meeting held at City Hall to consider the propriety of advising the city council to make an investment of £100,000 (in lottery tickets) to aid the financing of the Toronto and Lake Huron Railway. Although some argued that lotteries were a "debasing and demoralizing influence," the meeting recommended that the city support the scheme and the council in turn passed a by-law to that effect, subject to the approval of the voters. The vote was held on June 3rd and 4th. An early yet resounding affirmation of Toronto the "GOOD" was reflected in the fact that only 196 of the 865 votes supported the scheme. Gurnett resigned from the city council at the end of 1850, after having been appointed the first police magistrate of Toronto. As evidence of how much his image, and perhaps his temperament, had mellowed, he was chosen by none other then his earlier opponent, Robert Baldwin. He served in this position, apparently with some distinction, until his death on November 17th, 1861.

Whether his ardent support of the powerful "Family Compact" was based on ambition or ideology, Gurnett was undoubtedly one of the founders of the city. He was a man of administrative abilities which he devoted almost exclusively to the betterment of the city.

JOHN POWELL, lawyer and politician; b. 19 June 1809 at Niagara, the son of John and Isabella Powell (*née* Shaw, daughter of General Aeneas Shaw), and grandson of Chief Justice William Dummer Powell; m. August 1830 Eleanor Drean, and they had 8 children; d. 24 February 1881 at St Catharines, Ontario.

JOHN POWELL
MAYOR 1838-40

On the night of December 4th, 1837, as the followers of William Lyon Mackenzie (q.v.) gathered at Montgomery's Tavern, John Powell and Archibald Macdonald decided to "ride up Yonge Street Road to gather what information they could." Officials and residents of the city had heard only rumours of an impending invasion by Mackenzie's rebels and, borrowing Sheriff W. B. Jarvis's prize horse "Charley" and a brace of pistols, Powell set off up Yonge Street to reconnoitre. In the vicinity of "Gallows Hill" Powell and his companion were captured by a rebel patrol led by Mackenzie himself, who ordered the captives escorted to rebel headquarters. Soon after, however, Powell withdrew his pistols from under his coat, shot his guard (Captain John Anderson) in the back of the head, and, wheeling his horse, frantically made his escape. Moments later, on his way toward the city he again encountered Mackenzie and riding up to the rebel leader, "fired point blank into Mackenzie's face." As fate would have it, the pistol misfired and Powell, not chancing a reload, made good his escape. Upon arrival in the city he warned the Lieutenant-Governor, Sir Francis Bond Head, of the rebel activity, which proved the death knell of the hopes of the rebel army. Powell's exploits on this night did much to further his already successful career. A notable member of the "Family Compact" and a lawyer since 1835, he had practised law from his office on Toronto's fashionable King Street.

29

In 1837 he had been elected alderman for St Andrew's Ward and appointed to the influential finance and assessment committee. A month after the collapse of Mackenzie's rebellion in December 1837, however, he was not only returned as alderman for St Andrew's but proclaimed "the saviour of the city," and at the age of 28, was the council's unanimous choice for Mayor.

During his first year as Mayor, Powell presided over a council preoccupied with such matters as posting sentries around the city, organizing militia units in the wards, and expanding the permanent police establishment to 12 men. Powell was again chosen Mayor in 1839 and 1840, though the latter contest was a heated one: four other candidates were nominated and a total of 10 polls was necessary to secure his election. Reelected alderman in 1841, Powell attended council infrequently and finally in September submitted his resignation. He continued to reside in Toronto, serving as a judge of the Home District court until 1844 when he accepted the position of registrar of Lincoln County. In this capacity, he removed to Niagara, and later St Catharines, where he lived quietly, probably on the family estate.

John Powell the first member of the "Family Compact" to be Mayor, left no unforgettable mark on the affairs of the city government. Nevertheless, during his three terms as Mayor, important civic issues were raised and decided. For example, in 1840 the province deeded to the city lakefront waterlots, the later development of which would produce the Esplanade. At the same time, serious overtures began regarding the building of municipal services such as gas and water supply systems; services becoming absolutely essential to a city whose population by 1840 had grown to more than 13,000. But these were achievements of the council in general, rather than of the Mayor. John Powell's fame was a personal one, albeit dramatic and much applauded at the time, achieved by his own daring on the eve of the rebellion of 1837.

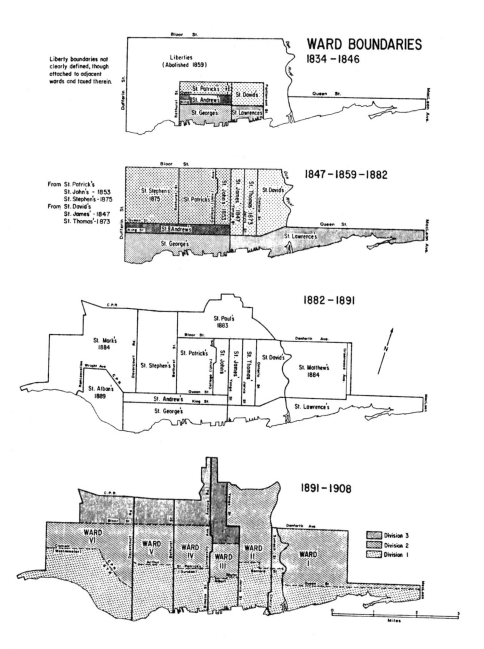

WARD BOUNDARIES
1834 – 1846

Liberty boundaries not
clearly defined, though
attached to adjacent
wards and taxed therein.

Liberties
(Abolished 1859)

Bloor St.
Queen St.

St. Patricks
St. Andrews
St. Davids
St. Georges
St. Lawrences

1847 – 1859 – 1882

From St. Patrick's
   St. John's - 1853
   St. Stephen's - 1875
From St. David's
   St. James' - 1847
   St. Thomas'- 1873

Bloor St.
St. Stephen's 1875
St. Patricks
St. John's 1853
St. James' 1847
St. Thomas 1873
St. David's
Queen St.
St. Andrews
St. George's
St. Lawrence's

1882 – 1891

C.P.R.
St. Paul's 1883
Bloor St.
Danforth Ave.
St. Mark's 1884
St. Patrick's
St. John's
St. Thomas
St. David's
St. Stephen's
St. Matthew's 1884
St. Alban's 1889
Queen St.
St. Andrew's   King St.
St. George's
St. Lawrence's

1891 – 1908

C.P.R.
Bloor St.
Danforth Ave.
WARD VI
WARD V
WARD IV
WARD III
WARD II
WARD I

Division 3
Division 2
Division 1

Miles

31

GEORGE MONRO, merchant and politician; b. 1801 in Scotland; d. 5 January 1878 in Toronto.

GEORGE MONRO
MAYOR 1841

Toronto's sixth chief magistrate or Mayor was George Monro. Born in Scotland, he had come to Upper Canada with his family and settled in Niagara about 1802. By 1815 young George was working in the retail grocery store of John Young in York. Early demonstrating his considerable business acumen, Monro soon became a partner, but he later dissolved that business and formed a wholesale dry goods company on King Street East with his older brother John. In 1824 the brothers separated, George becoming one of the most successful merchants in York.

As a young and successful businessman, he took an active part in the social life of the community; a pewholder at St James Cathedral, he was a member of the Bible Society and the Church Society. His business success also led to involvement in other ventures, and subsequently he held directorships in the Home District Savings Bank, the Bank of British North America, and the British America Assurance Company. Monro had always taken his civic duties seriously, serving as a magistrate for the town of York in 1833. In 1834 he was elected to the first city council as alderman for St Lawrence Ward, an office he filled until 1845 (except for 1836). In 1841 he was chosen Mayor after the nomination of George Gurnett (q.v.) was narrowly defeated, apparently because of the recently disclosed impropriety of Mr Gurnett in renting a house to one of the city's notorious madames. In any case, Monro presided over a

33

council during a period of intense activity. On February 6th, 1841 Toronto heard the devastating announcement that the capital of the newly united Province of Canada was to be Kingston. Torontonians viewed this news as ruinous, few disagreeing with the despairing remark that "grass would soon grow in the streets." The Mayor and city council sent the requisite petitions of protest, arguing that the capital should at least alternate between Toronto and Quebec City. However serious the psychological impact of the loss of the seat of government was, it soon became apparent that the city had not been dealt a fatal economic blow. Robert Stanton, the Queen's Printer, optimistically observed that the "village certainly begins to wear the appearance of a deserted one. Yet there are many new buildings going up and very large supplies of goods coming into it." Indeed, when the city council turned to the business of municipal affairs it accomplished much in the way of local improvements during Monro's tenure. In mid 1841 the corporation concluded negotiations with a Montreal-based group led by Albert Furniss, to begin construction of gas street lighting. The act of parliament which incorporated the newly formed gas company also contained provision for the establishment of waterworks.

In general, however, provincial politics continued to dominate the city, and in fact Monro found himself not only Mayor, but also a candidate for one of the Toronto seats in the new legislative assembly. Running on a Tory ticket with Henry Sherwood (q.v.), Monro managed to poll the fewest votes, the reformers winning both seats. When the results were known, much violence ensued. "Intelligence of Broken heads and arms was received from various quarters." In the end at least one man was killed. Though he completed his term as Mayor, a provincial investigation later chastised Monro for failure to keep the peace, the first obligation of the city's chief magistrate.

In 1844 Monro was to make another attempt to enter the legislature, this time standing in the east riding of York. He was defeated again but after successfully challenging his opponent's qualifications, he was declared elected and sat in the house until the next year. In 1848 he retired from politics after losing yet another electoral contest, this time to a candidate, William Hume Blake, who was in Europe at the time of the election. In 1857 Monro retired from business and spent most of his time devoted to his great love of plants and flowers. His house and gardens at Front and George Streets were for many years a landmark of the city and, after his death, became the well-known The Black Horse Inn.

HENRY SHERWOOD, lawyer and politician; b. 1807 in Augusta, Upper Canada, eldest son of Livius Peters and Charlotte Sherwood (*née* Jones, daughter of Jonas Jones); m. 22 July 1829 Mary Graham Smith, daughter of Peter Smith of Kingston; d. 7 July 1855 at Kissinger, Bavaria.

HENRY SHERWOOD
MAYOR 1842-44

Henry Sherwood, Toronto's seventh Mayor, was a man of high social standing and much ability. Born a member of a prominent Brockville family which was allied with the "Family Compact," he received his early education at the Home District Grammar School under the tutelage of the venerable John Strachan, later lord bishop of Toronto. Sherwood went on to study law and was called to the bar in 1828 before setting up his practice in Brockville.

Sherwood's involvement in politics had actually begun at the tender age of 19, when he had been one of the "Tory" youths responsible for wrecking the newspaper offices of William Lyon Mackenzie (q.v.). Not long after opening his law office in Brockville, young Sherwood ran in the provincial elections of 1830, finishing last. Undaunted he ran again in 1834 and though he faired better, he lost again. The ambitious Sherwood finally won the seat in the assembly for the town of Brockville in the election of 1836, holding the riding until 1840.

In the first election following the union of the Canadas in 1841 he was nominated for Toronto. He had, in fact, moved his legal practice to Toronto some six years previously, and along with his running mate, Mayor George Monro (q.v.), was counting upon anti-union Tory support from the city. This support did not materialize as both were soundly defeated in what can only be described as one of the more riot filled elections in Toronto's history. Following this defeat, Sherwood moved into municipal politics, being elected as alderman for St David's Ward. When the council met in January 1842, Sherwood was chosen Mayor. But like his predecessor and ally, George Monro, he remained much involved in provincial politics. Indeed, during his first term as Mayor he was sworn in as solicitor general of Canada in July by Governor General Sir Charles Bagot, though he was excluded from the cabinet the following September. Similarly during his second mayoralty, to which he had been elected in 1843, he became involved in the March by-elections. He won the Toronto seat and was again gazetted solicitor general. Retaining the mayoralty in 1844 Sherwood fought and won yet another provincial election that year.

Surprisingly enough, Sherwood seems to have been a popular and effective Mayor. No doubt most of the credit belongs to the committees which were responsible for regulating the market, paving the streets, collecting the taxes and the like. In 1842, for example, the standing committee on gas and water proudly reported that a waterworks was under way and that 94 gas lights were illuminating King and Yonge Streets. But some of the credit does belong to Mayor Sherwood, who worked assiduously in the standing committees and, having a sound knowledge of procedures, presided with surprising moderation and fairness over a quickly growing civic government.

In fact, during Sherwood's final term as Mayor, it became apparent that the corporation had outgrown its accommodation in the St Lawrence Market. A select committee was established to receive plans for the construction of Toronto's first municipal offices. Mayor Sherwood presided over the meeting in March 1844 at which the committee report was adopted which recommended the acceptance of Henry Bower Lane's drawings and design. The construction of the new City Hall began in the summer after the purchase of the Home District Farmers' Storehouse at Jarvis and Front Streets had provided the site. Mayor Sherwood no doubt happily presided over the festivities during the cornerstone laying in September.

After his final mayoralty term in 1844, Sherwood continued to sit on the city council until 1849. He also continued to be involved in the provincial scene. On May 29th, 1847 he became attorney general of Canada West, the head of what proved to be an interim ministry. Typical of the unsettled political climate, he was to hold this office for only eight weeks. He continued in and out of parliament for the next few years, losing in 1851 and winning in 1853 only to lose again in 1854. In the summer of 1855 Sherwood undertook a European holiday to aid his failing health. He died in Kissinger, Bavaria, on July 7th, 1855 at the early age of 48.

WILLIAM HENRY BOULTON, lawyer and politician; b. 19 April 1812 in York (Toronto), the son of D'Arcy (Jr) and Sarah Ann Boulton (*née* Robinson, daughter of Sir John Beverley Robinson); m. Harriette Elizabeth Dixon (who later married Goldwin Smith); d. 15 February 1874 in Toronto.

WILLIAM HENRY BOULTON
MAYOR 1845-47, 1858

When the council met for the first time in 1845 to elect a Mayor, the choice of the majority was William Henry Boulton. According to tradition, the Mayor-elect was to be conducted to the chair where he took the oath of office and returned thanks to the council, but Boulton was not present at the meeting and tradition was broken. In Montreal attending a session of the legislative assembly as member for Toronto, Boulton did not return to the city to take up his duties until February 1845.

Unlike his predecessor, however, Mayor Boulton's involvement in provincial politics was less the result of driving ambition than of obligations inherent in his social position. William Henry Boulton was born into one of the leading families of Upper Canada: his grandfather, D'Arcy Boulton Sr, was chief justice of Upper Canada, and his family (a bevy of lawyers, judges, and politicians) also included such luminaries as his father, D'Arcy Boulton Jr, and his uncles George Strange Boulton, Henry John Boulton, and John Beverley Robinson. Following family tradition, William had studied law. Called to the bar at the age of 23, he had joined the prestigious Toronto firm of Gamble and Boulton.

Consistent with his standing as a "gentleman", Boulton was very active in social life of the community, and his estate, the Grange, was often the centre of early Toronto's social gatherings. He was a founder and director of the original Toronto Club and in

1840 was treasurer of the association which held the two-day Toronto Races. Organized horse-racing meets had been held as early as 1837 on the property owned by John Scarlett, northwest of the city, known as Runnymede. In 1841 and 1843 the races were actually held on the spacious grounds adjoining the Grange. On another occasion, in 1846, Boulton hosted the organizational meeting of the first Toronto lodge of the Independent Order of Oddfellows and was elected the lodge's first grand noble. Boulton also served many years as an active member of the Orange Lodge, eventually being elected Deputy Grand Master of British North America.

It would be wrong, however, to suggest that Boulton was a mere cipher as a member of parliament or as Mayor. Indeed, he was a man of much ability, especially as an orator, and of strong opinions.

As member of parliament for Toronto from 1844 to 1853, he variously supported conservatives William Henry Draper and Henry Sherwood (q.v.). During these years he acted as the self-appointed and unequivocal defender of the preferred position of the Church of England, especially with regard to education and the clergy reserves. Similarly, he was an energetic civic politician. Serving as alderman for St Patrick's Ward from 1838 until 1842 he attended council regularly and served as a member of various important committees: board of health, police and prisons, affairs of the market block, and board of works.

Returning to civic politics in 1844 after a two-year absence, he served again as alderman for St Patrick's Ward until 1847 and was elected Mayor for three terms, from 1845 to 1847. Characteristically, he brought much prestige to the mayoralty and, although a Tory, was not averse to supporting enterprising endeavours such as the City of Toronto and Lake Huron Railway. Closely related to railway development was immigration, and in April 1847 Mayor Boulton chaired a meeting at City Hall assembled for the formation of an immigrant aid society. The list of those in attendance reads like a "who's who" of Toronto's political, religious, business and social elites. At the conclusion of the meeting it was decided to form the Emigrant Settlement Society and Boulton was unanimously thanked for "having called this meeting, and for his kindness and urbanity in presiding at the same."

During his third term as Mayor, he was to host Governor General Lord Elgin during his official visit to Toronto. The Mayor lavishly entertained the governor at the Grange, and even though the two men had little, if any, personal amiability toward each other, the spendour and dignity of the occasion impressed almost everyone. Unfortunately, one group which remained unimpressed was the finance and assessment committee of the city council. It seems that Mayor Boulton had taken it upon himself to spend £120 on the construction of triumphal arches, traditional for visiting royalty, to decorate the streets — an expenditure not, the committee reminded the Mayor, approved by council.

All this aside, the highlight of Boulton's mayoralty must have been the opening of the new City Hall at Front and Jarvis Streets. The civic government (with 13 standing committees) had grown substantially since 1834, and for some years had suffered from lack of space in the town hall in the St Lawrence Market Building. In the summer of 1845 the council began holding its meetings in its spacious new chamber, and by the end of the summer the corporation's officers, including city clerk, city chamberlain and city engineer, had also moved in to their new offices, their home for the next 54 years.

After his mayoralty ended in 1847, Boulton sat on council as alderman in 1852 and 1858, again being elected Mayor in 1858. During his tenure, intense negotiations were concluded with the province over the distribution of judicial powers between the province, the county, and the city. By this time the Mayor and aldermen had ceased to act as magistrates and cases were heard by the recorder or the police magistrate. In the turmoil, he resigned his mayoralty in a fight with the chief constable, Samuel Sherwood. He than ran for Mayor in January 1859 in the first mayoralty election by popular vote, but lost to the Reformer, Adam Wilson (q.v.).

Boulton then retired from politics and lived quietly in the stately Grange. Generally considered a competent public administrator, he had apparently neglected his private affairs and spent his later life sorting them out. After his death his wife continued to live at the Grange, and when she married the famous author Goldwin Smith in 1875 the Grange again became a centre of civic life. Today the Grange is a showpiece of the Art Gallery of Ontario.

JOHN GEORGE BOWES, merchant and politician; b. 1812 in Ireland; d. 20 May 1864 in Toronto.

JOHN GEORGE BOWES
MAYOR 1851-53, 1861-63

John George Bowes, Toronto's ninth Mayor, was born about 1812 near Clones, County Monaghan, Ireland. He arrived in York when about 21 and found employment in a dry goods store at 181 King Street East owned by Samuel E. Taylor. In 1840 Bowes and his brother-in-law, John Hall, were able to purchase the well-established firm of Buchanan, Harris and Company, at the corner of Yonge and Wellington. The business, renamed Bowes and Hall, flourished over the next 10 years, soon becoming the most successful wholesale dry goods operation of its time. By 1851 Bowes was sole owner of the business, which during that year had an assessed value of more than £100,000.

A genial Irishman, Bowes was a popular figure around Toronto, with a reputation as a man of the people, despite his ever-increasing wealth. He was a barrel-chested man of notable physical prowess who, it was said, was "an ugly customer in a row." Consistent with the turbulent politics of the day, it was well reported that he was not averse to mixing it up, although on more than one occasion "Mayor Bowes got a broken head."

Successful and popular, it was only natural that he become involved in civic affairs, and in November 1847 he accepted an appointment of the city council to the first Board of Trustees for the Common Schools. From 1850 to 1853 he was alderman in St James's Ward, and from 1851 to 1853 was chosen Mayor by the council. As

Mayor, Bowes combined his flamboyant style, public popularity, and public office to help the city usher in the railway era on an optimistic note. One old Toronto citizen later recalled the event:

> I remember witnessing the ceremony which took place on the bank on the South side of Front Street, just west of Simcoe Street, of the inauguration of the Ontario, Simcoe and Huron Railway (afterwards known as the Northern Railway). The first sod was turned, in the presence of a very large and interested crowd by Lady Elgin, who used a handsome silver spade and threw a little earth into a wheelbarrow which Mayor Bowes, who assisted in the ceremony, wheeled away a short distance and emptied. Mayor Bowes, who was one of Toronto's best and most popular mayors, and was elected six times to that position, had a great idea of the dignity and importance of his office and appeared in his cocked hat, sword, knee breeches and silk stockings.

During his third term, however, this optimism was shaken when Bowes was implicated, along with Sir Francis Hincks, attorney-general of Canada West, in the notorious "Ten Thousand Pound Job." The facts about the "job" were slow in coming to light but once they did it was discovered to the horror of some of his enemies and the horrified glee of others that Hincks and Bowes had turned a profit of £10,000 in a complicated deal which involved buying and selling city debentures. Worst of all, both had used information obtained from their respective offices. The city council investigated the situation and reported that although the Mayor could be accused of "lack of candour" he had done nothing illegal. In a subsequent stormy name-calling council meeting Bowes's supporters stood firm and several motions of censure were defeated, causing eight members of council to resign. The outraged oposition, however, pressed the case in the courts. Although finding Bowes innocent of any wrong-doing *per se*, owing to his public office it was argued that he had not acted totally for the public good by turning such a handsome profit. The court ordered him to pay back the money, which he did.

Following the outbreak of the controversy, Bowes withdrew from civic politics, but not as a defeated man. Indeed his

46

popularity, though somewhat weakened, was basically intact, and in the 1854 provincial elections he led the polls for one of the Toronto seats, defeating two former Mayors, Henry Sherwood (q.v.) and William Henry Boulton (q.v.). Bowes held this seat until 1858; and in 1856 he was re-elected to council as alderman for St David's Ward. In 1861 he used a lavish "pork barrel" campaign to return as Toronto's Mayor, who by this time was elected by popular vote, and was easily re-elected in 1862 and 1863. During these three years as Mayor, Bowes applied his experience in business and railways to the fast-growing finances of the city. A special committee of council under chairman Alfred Brunel was appointed to "take stock of the corporation's financial position." In January 1862 they reported that by the end of the year the city debt would more than $2½ million, of which more than 1 million was invested in railways and the Esplanade.

During his mayoralty, Bowes also had the opportunity to get involved in the planning, construction and opening of a railway of another kind — a street railway. In typical Bowes fashion, he was also personally involved in its finances, at one time holding the controlling shares. The street railway, consisting of six miles of track, was officially opened in September 1861 with a suitable celebration, including excursions up Yonge Street by city council.

In January 1864 Bowes was nominated for a 7th term but in the ensuing election he was narrowly defeated by Francis Henry Medcalf (q.v.). A few months later, Bowes died at his home in the city.

JOSHUA GEORGE BEARD, merchant and politician; b. 1797 in England; d. 9 November 1866 in Toronto.

JOSHUA GEORGE BEARD
MAYOR 1854

The tenth man to be Mayor was a respected and well-known Toronto Businessman, Joshua George Beard. Born in England, he had come to Canada and settled upon York as the place to make his fortune. He was soon much involved in the business life of the small but growing community, and in very short order became the best known and most successful wharfinger and coal and wood merchant. His business, styled J.G. Beard and Sons, was situated at the foot of Jarvis Street adjacent to a large wharf and elevator which bore his name. Eventually Beard's investments in real estate, including Beard's Hotel, made him one of the largest property owners in the city.

It seems Beard always took an interest in public affairs, serving as sheriff's clerk for many years and as secretary of the town of York. In 1834, with the incorporation of the city, he was elected to the first city council in a by-election as a councilman for St Lawrence Ward. With the exception of four years, Beard represented this ward as councilman or alderman until his mayoralty, 20 years later. Indeed, Beard's longevity on council and his respectability were undoubtedly the major factors contributing to his being the unanimous choice for mayor in 1854. Council was still reeling from the effects of the disclosure of the "Ten Thousand Pound Job," and stability and proven financial ability were highly desirable attributes.

49

Beard's mayoralty, however, began inauspiciously for he was taken seriously ill in January 1854 and was not able to assume his duties for some months. In the interim, John Beverley Robinson (q.v.) was appointed president of council to act in his stead. Returning to council in April, Mayor Beard assumed his duties as presiding officer. For the remainder of his term, Beard appears to have fulfilled his duties admirably and, perhaps to everyone's relief, council managed to get through much of its regular business (public works — such as sewers — railway matters and the Esplanade) without a major scandal.

Beard did not seek re-election to city council in 1855 but did continue to take an active interest in another area of municipal politics with which he had long been associated: public schools. He had, in fact, been elected a member for St Lawrence Ward on the Board of Trustees since the board was established in 1850. Beard succeeded Dr Joseph Workman as chairman of the board in 1852 and held this office until forced to retire by ill health 12 years later. A supporter of Egerton Ryerson and an advocate of free education supported by municipal taxes (a contentious principle in the 1850's) Beard took an intense personal interest in the achievements of the school boards, seldom missing an opportunity to speak on behalf of these "new ideals." On one occasion during its formative years, when the school board was attempting to finance the construction of the first public-owned school, he co-signed a promissory note for £8,750 when the debentures issued could not be sold quickly enough. By 1864 the board had built 9 schools and the aggregate number on the registers was 5,550.

In 1864 Joshua Beard retired to private life because of poor health. For some years his sons had been conducting his business affairs and one served as councilman for St Lawrence Ward, 1865-66. Beard's death on November 9th 1866 was noted by city council with the passing of a resolution of "profound regret of the lamented demise of our old and respected citizen."

Toronto in 1854.

GEORGE WILLIAM ALLAN, lawyer and politician; b. 9 January 1822 in York (Toronto), the son of the Honorable William Allan; m. Louisa Maude Robinson (daughter of Sir John Beverley Robinson); d. 27 July 1901 in Toronto.

GEORGE WILLIAM ALLAN
MAYOR 1855

George William Allan was the eleventh man to fill the Mayor's chair. He had served briefly on council in 1849 as alderman for St David's Ward, being returned in a by-election in July of that year following the resignation of Dr Joseph Workman. He was returned in that capacity in 1854 and took a leading role in council and committee, being appointed to the all important standing committee on finance and assessment as well as the increasingly controversial committee on wharves and harbours. Appointed by council a commissioner of the Toronto Harbour Trust, Allan also served as the city's representative on the board of directors of the Ontario, Simcoe and Lake Huron Railway, and as such was delegated the responsibility of expediting the passage in the provincial parliament of the amended Esplanade Act.

Reelected alderman in 1855, Allan was the unanimous choice of the council for Mayor. A distinguished figure and competent administrator, Mayor Allan, and for that matter the entire council, spent much of their time defending the interests of the corporation as the railway boom reached its peak. Indeed, although he more than adequately discharged his ceremonial duties, Allan won the respect of all by energetically wading through the mire of negotiations and investigations caused by the construction of the railways and the Esplanade. When his mayoralty came to a close in

December, it was a sincere city council that passed an elaborate resolution of deep-felt appreciation.

Allan did not return to civic politics after 1855. He did, however, continue to lead a very active public life in the city. In fact, reading a list of his business investments, social involvements and political offices leaves one breathless:

> Chief Commisioner of the Canada Company, President of Western Canada Loan and Savings Company, Board of Directors of British America Insurance Company, Lieutenant-Colonel of the Regimental Division of East Toronto, Honorary Member of the Queen's Own Rifles, President of the Upper Canada Bible Society, Member of St Andrew's Society and Highland Society, President of Toronto Mechanic's Institute, Chancellor of the University of Trinity College, First President of the Toronto Conservatory of Music, Secretary and several times President of the Canadian Institute.

Two of Allan's more special interests were art and floriculture and he did much to promote the development of these interest in Toronto. For example, Allan did much to secure the reputation of Paul Kane by sponsoring the young artist's trip to the west and by purchasing many of the paintings completed at its conclusion. Allan later served as president of the Ontario Society of Artists and as chairman of the Art Union of Canada. Similarly Allan's interest in floriculture convinced him to donate to the city the 5 acres of gardens which later, expanded to 15 acres, became the Horticulture Garden or Allan Gardens. He served for 25 years as president of the Horticultural Society of Toronto.

A Fellow of the Royal Geographical Society and the Zoological Society, Allan travelled more extensively than any Upper Canadian of his time. From 1850 to 1853 he travelled widely in Europe (reportedly visiting every country) and extended his tour through Egypt and Asia. It was said that he was the first Canadian to stand at the summit of the Great Pyramid.

On top of this remarkable array of involvements, Allan remained an important political figure. In 1858 he was elected to the legislative council of Canada for the constituency of York. Serving until Confederation, Allan chaired the private bills committee. In 1867 he was nominated to the senate of Canada and in March 1888 he was elected speaker of the senate, serving until 1891 when he was appointed to the privy council.

G. W. Allan's career was as much a reflection of his social and financial standing as his interesting character. Born the only son of the wealthy Honorable William Allan, he had inherited the family fortune, including the impressive estate of "Moss Park." He had received a first class education at Upper Canada College and when studying law was articled to Clarke Gamble. Called to the bar in 1846, young Allan practised with James Lukin Robinson, eldest son and heir of Sir John Beverley Robinson. But privilege alone could not account for either the energy or the natural inquisitiveness that led him around the world.

JOHN BEVERLEY ROBINSON, lawyer, politician and Lieutenant-Governor of Ontario; b. 21 February 1820 in York (Toronto), the second son of Sir John Beverley Robinson; m. Mary Jane Hagerman (daughter of the Honourable Christopher Hagerman); d. in June 1896 in Toronto.

JOHN BEVERLEY ROBINSON
MAYOR 1856

John Beverley Robinson, Toronto's twelfth Mayor, was the second son and namesake of one of the most eminent figures in the early history of Upper Canada, Sir John Beverley Robinson. The elder Robinson was a man of considerable legal talent who served as solicitor-general, attorney-general, chief justice, and president of the court of appeal. After attending Upper Canada College, the younger Robinson, following his father's footsteps, studied law, first with Christopher A. Hagerman and later with James M. Strachan and John H. Cameron. Though called to the bar in 1844, Robinson was not entered on the Barrister's Roll or Attorney's Roll, the reasons being that his father and father-in-law were the two leading judges before whom he would have had to plead cases. Besides which, it appears that Robinson was little interested in court appearances.

Robinson was in fact much engaged in the entrepreneurial activities surrounding the promotion of railways, especially the Ontario, Simcoe and Huron Railway (later the Northern), and personally organized and spoke at numerous public meetings to urge Torontonians to support the proposed railway. Involvement in what Robinson called the "city railroad" led him into civic politics, and in 1851, 1853-54 and 1856-57 he was alderman for St Patrick's Ward. Once on council, Robinson worked assiduously for the railway interest, led the pro-railway forces on council and helped frame legislation under which the city invested heavily in railways. From January until July 1854, because of Mayor J. G. Beard's (q.v.) absence due to illness, Robinson served as president of the city council and during the year was appointed the city's representative on the board of director's of the Northern. Later in his career, Robinson was to serve for a number of years as president of that railway.

It was most appropriate that in 1856 Robinson be elected Mayor. In that year another great railway event took place — the completion of the Toronto to Montreal section of the Grand Trunk Railway. Mayor Robinson led ten specially appointed cars of civic officials to attend the mammoth celebration sponsored by the city of Montreal.

During his mayoralty, Robinson did of course turn his attention to matters other than railways. Steps were taken to acquire the waterworks which, still in private hands, was clearly not fulfilling its contract to provide an adequate supply of water to the city. In 1856 the council also purchased from Dr Scadding a Don River lot as a site for a jail and industrial farm. The Mayor was called upon to perform the usual ceremonial duties and one of the more interesting ones was the civic reception held to honour the homecoming of Major Frederick Wells of the 1st Royals. Wells was a Toronto native who had been awarded the Legion of Honour by the Emperor of France for actions in the Crimean War. The city council voted the sum of £100 to purchase a sword of honour to be presented to Wells by the Mayor on behalf of the city.

Following his mayoralty, Robinson sat as a member of parliament until 1880, serving briefly in 1862 as president of the council in Cartier-Macdonald administration. In parliament, Robinson played a leading role as Toronto's representative, especially concerning railway matters. In recognition of the need to maintain a close watch on the city's parliamentary interest the city council formalized Robinson's role in parliament by appointing him city solicitor in 1864. He served in this capacity until he retired from the house in 1880.

Although Robinson's recognized successes in parliament were primarily related to Toronto and railways, one other stands out. In 1861, with the blessing of the crown lands office, Robinson travelled to England to attempt to sell to English subscribers a tract of land of over 1,000,000 acres. Prior to his departure the scheme met with more than a little scepticism. Once there, however, Robinson worked assiduously and, drawing upon his father's contacts, managed to sell the land to a company which included the former lieutenant-governor of Upper Canada, Sir Francis Bond Head, and a future prime minister of England, Lord Salisbury. Upon his return to Toronto, Robinson's efforts were much acclaimed.

In 1880 Robinson was appointed lieutenant-governor of Ontario, a position which he was to fill with much dignity and enthusiasm. A distinguished figure of little more than average height but of splendid physique, Robinson had excelled in athletics as a youth, being considered at one time the best boxer in the city. He remained interested in sports throughout his life and was president of the Toronto Cricket Club, a member of the Toronto Gymnastic and Fencing Club, and a founder of the Toronto Athletic Club. Mrs Robinson, daughter of Christopher Hagerman, was a popular figure in her own right, being a recognized and accomplished vocalist who often gave concerts, always for charitable causes. An extremely popular couple, they performed their vice-regal duties until his retirement in 1887. John Beverley Robinson died suddenly in June 1896 while attending a political meeting in Massey Hall.

JOHN HUTCHISON, merchant and politician; b. 1817 in Scotland; d. 7 July 1863 at Metis (Quebec).

JOHN HUTCHISON
MAYOR 1857

John Hutchison, Toronto's thirteenth Mayor, had been a resident of the city for less than a decade when he entered office. Born in Port Patrick, Wigtonshire, Scotland in 1817, he was brought to Montreal by his parents in 1828. There he worked in the famous Montreal mercantile firm of Torrance and Company, where he appears to have shown an excellent aptitude for business. In 1847 he came to Toronto and opened an office at Church near Front Street, styled Hutchison, Black and Co., a commission merchant operation that relied heavily upon his Montreal business connections.

During his 10-year sojourn, however, Hutchison did take an active part in the social, political, and business affairs of the city. Finding the Toronto market a reasonably lucrative one, Hutchison was soon investing in numerous local enterprises. He was a director and shareholder of the Toronto and Sarnia Railroad Company; a director of the Metropolitan Building Company and of the Metropolitan Gas and Water Company. Not surprisingly, considering his Scottish origin, Hutchison was involved in the early years of the Toronto Curling Club, serving as that organization's secretary-treasurer.

Soon after his arrival Hutchison also became involved in municipal politics, serving as alderman for St James's Ward in 1853. During this term in office, he was an outspoken critic of Mayor

Bowes (q.v.) and the implications of the "Ten Thousand Pound Job," and was one of the aldermen who resigned in protest when city council failed to censure Bowes for his conduct. In 1856, Hutchison returned to council as alderman for St James's and, probably in recognition of his business acumen, council elected him chairman of the finance and assessment committee, to all intents and purposes the executive committee of council. During his tenure as chairman of this committee Hutchison made a reputation for himself as an astute manager of funds and often criticized his fellow members of council for their lack of thriftiness. In that year he was also chairman of the committee to investigate the salaries and duties of the civic officials, and recommended several unpopular reforms. Of more popular issue were the repeated, if unsuccessful, attempts of the finance committee, led by Hutchison, to reduce local taxes.

By 1857 the young man from Montreal had earned a solid local following, and in the aldermanic election in St James's Ward he was easily re-elected. When the council-elect met in January to choose its presiding officer, as was customary at the first meeting of the year, they had a more serious problem on the table. During the municipal elections, a riot had broken out in St David's Ward and a "mob" had taken over the polling station. The poll clerk reported that he had been prevented from taking a complete poll of the electors and was unable to make a correct legal return. Consequently, there were no representatives for St David's Ward at the meeting and this raised the question of the legality of the council proceeding, especially with regard to choosing a Mayor. The astute city clerk, Charles Daly, had foreseen the possibility of such questions being raised and had sought legal advice from, amongst others, the city solicitor, Clarke Gamble, and the attorney general, John A. Macdonald. Moreover, although legal opinion varied as to detail, there was a consensus that council should proceed with choosing representatives for St David's Ward and then the Mayor. After a meeting that stretched to three in the morning, the council had accomplished its first task; then, on a motion by Oliver Mowat, a tired and befuddled council chose Hutchison as Mayor, by the slim majority of one.

Hutchisons's term as Mayor was hectic indeed. Through the first half of the 1850s the city had embarked in numerous large public works which, combined with the city's ever-increasing involvement in railways, brought a crush of business to council. Several times during the year, motions were made by various aldermen to increase the number of council meetings and eliminate the introduction of new business until the backlog was cleared up. While city council attempted to focus on the regular business of running the city, major issues such as railways and the Esplanade dominated debate, leaving the bulk of business untouched.

Generally speaking, 1857 marked the end of the orgy of development connected with the railway era. City council taking a more adversary approach to railway developers was no longer willing to freely subsidize every scheme. Reformers such as Adam Wilson (q.v.) led the assault on give-aways to railways and demanded more representation on the railways' boards of directors to protect the interests of the city. This new approach caused serious confrontations which led amongst other things to the resignation of the city engineer, who claimed he could simply not keep up with the work, and eventually to the cancellation of the Esplanade contract.

Added to all of this, Hutchison found himself Mayor of a city that was suffering from the most dramatic economic depression the province had ever experienced. One contemporary later observed:

1857 will long be remembered as the gloomiest epoch in the history of the commerce and industries of the country. Solvency and enterprise seemed to be things of the past. Mercantile houses of long established reputation went by the board; the factories were idle, trade was stagnant, and the streets swarmed with beggars and vagrants. Even those who had hitherto been in ordinarily comfortable circumstances now tasted for the first time the bitterness of poverty, and there is reason to believe that not a few deaths from starvation occurred. As usual, in such times of depression, drunkenness was rife, and during the year close upon two thousand people were committed to gaol.

As economic matters worsened in late fall of 1857, the Mayor himself fell victim to the crash:

Toronto November 2 1857

To the Presiding Alderman
Toronto City Council
Toronto

In consequence of the temporary derangement of the affairs of my firm, I feel it due to the Citizens of Toronto and to myself that I should resign my office as Mayor of the City and I will thank you to communicate my resignation to the Council this evening.

The shortness of the period now to elapse before the annual election raised a doubt as to the expediency of this course but I felt that under the circumstances I ought not to hesitate and moreover that my whole time and energies ought to be devoted for some weeks to the readjustment of my private affairs.

Hutchison was persuaded by a deputation of council to remain in office until the expiration of his term; but by the beginning of the next year he had vacated his storehouses and offices and left for to Montreal never to return to Toronto. Five years later a *Globe* obituary noted his death at Métis (Quebec) after retiring there because of poor health.

Hutchison & Co., Wellington Street, north side — east of Yonge, 1856. One year later, during his Mayoralty, John Hutchison went bankrupt. (PAC ref. PA 122974)

DAVID BREAKENRIDGE READ, lawyer, politician and historian; b. 13 June 1823 in Augusta (Ontario); the son of John Landon and Janet Read (*née* Breakenridge); d. 11 May 1904 in Toronto.

DAVID BREAKENRIDGE READ
MAYOR 1858

David Breakenridge Read, the fourteenth man to serve as chief magistrate, has the dubious distinction of serving the shortest term of office in the history of the city. Read was elected interim Mayor by council on November 11th, 1858, following the resignation of Mayor W. H. Boulton (q.v.), and served only till December. Moreover, although he had taken an active part in the proceedings of council, sitting on various standing and select committees, Read was serving only his first term on council. At the end of his brief term, Read declined to be further involved in the world of municipal politics and returned to his law practice.

It would, however, be an injustice to Read to belittle his talents, abilities, and accomplishments because of his being somewhat of a cipher as Mayor. Born of United Empire Loyalist parents in Augusta (Ontario), he was educated at Upper Canada College, studied law in Brockville and Toronto and was called to the bar in 1845. He practised law in Toronto with numerous prominent partners, establishing a substantial and learned reputation. Elected a bencher of the law Society in November 1855, he remained active in this capacity for more than 25 years. In recognition of his abilities, he was also appointed a commissioner for consolidating the statutes of Upper Canada in 1856, and a Q C in 1858.

D. B. Read, apart from his professional activities, involved himself in a number of social organizations including the Toronto Club, the Royal Canadian Yacht Club, The Toronto Cricket Club and the Caer Howell Bowling Club, of which he was for many years honourary president.

Upon his retirement from professional life in 1881, Read studiously pursued his interest in local history. He was a member of the Ontario Historical Society and president of the York Pioneers. His enthusiasm led to the publication of numerous books, including *Lives of the Judges of Upper Canada* (1889), *The Life and Times of General John Graves Simcoe* (1890), *The Life and Times of Maj. General Sir Isaac Brock* (1894), *The Rebellion of 1837* (1896), and *The Lieutenant-Governors of Upper Canada and Ontario* (1900). Read died at his residence on Breadalbane Street in Toronto on May 11th 1904, at the age of 8l.

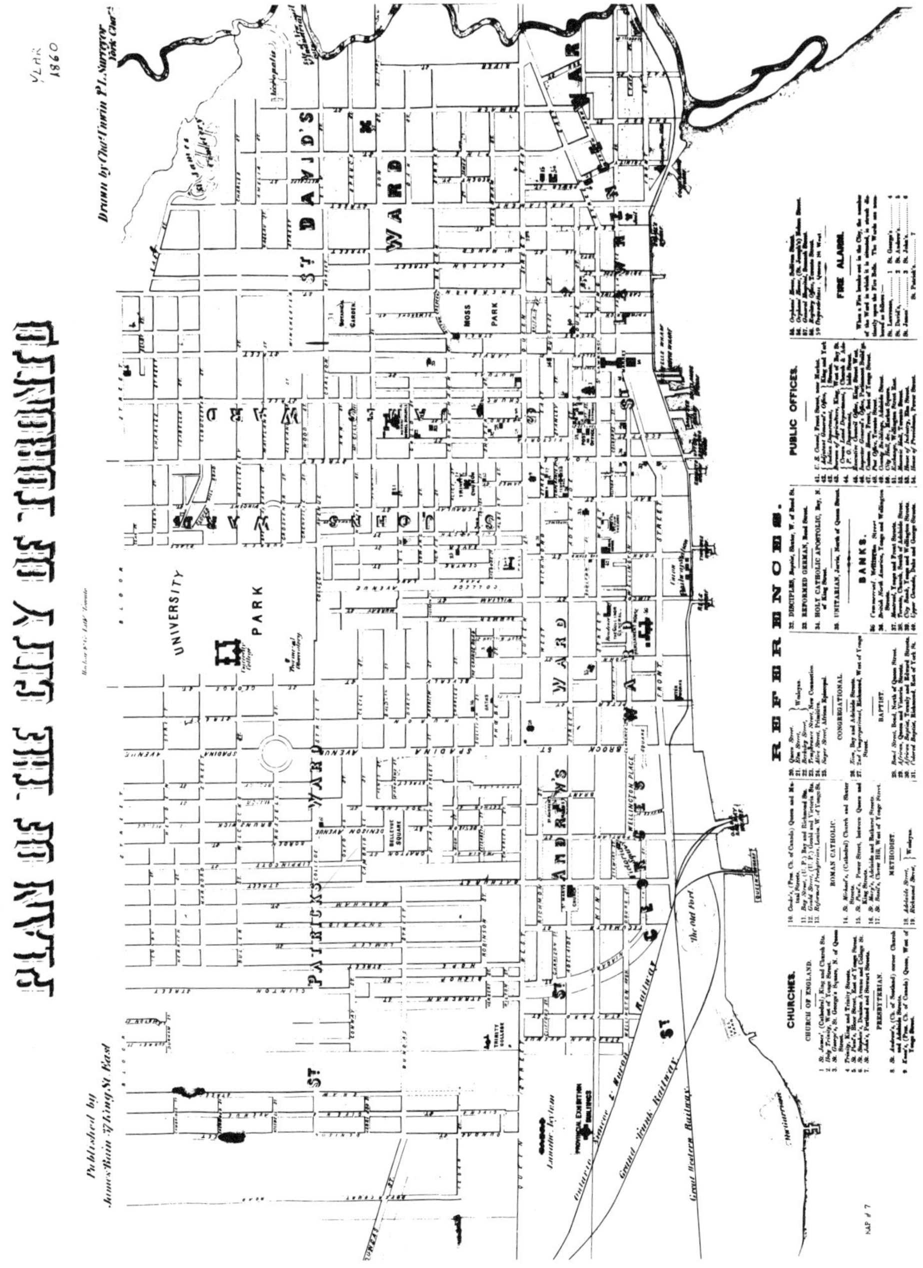

PLAN OF THE CITY OF TORONTO

1860

Drawn by Chas Unwin Pl. Surveyor

Published by James Ross, King St East

ST DAVID'S WARD

ST JOHN'S WARD

ST PATRICK'S WARD

ST ANDREW'S WARD

ST JAMES'S WARD

UNIVERSITY PARK

MOSS PARK

REFERENCES.

CHURCHES.

CHURCH OF ENGLAND.

PRESBYTERIAN.

ROMAN CATHOLIC.

CONGREGATIONAL.

BAPTIST.

METHODIST.

PUBLIC OFFICES.

BANKS.

FIRE ALARM.

SIR ADAM WILSON, lawyer, judge and politician; b. 22 September 1814 in Scotland; d. 28 December 1891 in Toronto.

SIR ADAM WILSON
MAYOR 1859-60

Toronto's fifteenth Mayor was Adam Wilson. Born in Scotland, he had come to Upper Canada as a youth to work for an uncle in Halton County. In January 1834 young Wilson moved to Toronto where he began the study of law in the offices of Robert Baldwin Sullivan (q.v.) and Robert Baldwin. Called to the bar in 1839, Wilson formed a partnership with Baldwin and established a large practice in Toronto. Wilson's legal abilities earned him an appointment as a bencher of the Law Society and a QC in 1850.

An ardent reformer by affiliation and inclination, Wilson entered municipal politics in 1855 as alderman for St Patrick's Ward. Once on council, he soon assumed leadership of a faction which strongly opposed the railway interests that had long dominated council proceedings. More specifically, Wilson and his colleagues focused their attack on the previous council's handling of the Esplanade project. This was a plan to fill in about 500 feet of the waterfront, thereby producing an Esplanade or terrace along the lake and to provide waterfront access to downtown for the proposed railways. The contract for the construction of the Esplanade, from Spadina to the Don River, was awarded to a consortium led by Casimir S. Gzowski, David L. Macpherson, Alexander T. Galt, men who also had large interests in the railways. Construction had begun in 1853 and proceeded slowly until 1855 when rumours of graft and mismanagement were rampant. The outspoken Wilson took up the cause, charging that the contractors were being paid too much for the amount of work being completed: further, he accused the contractor of deliberately overestimating the required work in order to pocket the difference. Although the consortium fought back, Wilson managed to demonstrate to council that all was not well and the contract with Gzowski *et al.* was cancelled. Again the contractors fought back, threatening legal action against the city, but when Wilson agreed that the courtoom was an appropriate place to examine what had really gone on, the group declined to pursue the matter.

Wilson won considerable local popularity and support during these skirmishes but his recognized legal talents took him away from municipal politics in 1856, when he was appointed a commissioner for the consolidation of the statues of Upper Canada. He returned to the municipal scene in 1859. Pursuant to an act of parliament of 1858, the choice of the Mayor for 1859 was to be by a general vote of the electors and not by the aldermen as in previous years. Consequently, on December 20th, 1858, the city clerk, Charles Daly, convened a public meeting in front of City Hall for the purpose of nominating candidates. Three men were nominated, John George Bowes (q.v.), William Henry Boulton (q.v.), and A. Wilson. Wilson's campaign centred on railway give-aways and poor management by previous councils in dealing with the railways. On the other hand, Bowes and Boulton, were both former mayors and deeply involved in railways. The election, which took place on January 3rd and 4th, 1859, produced convincing results: Boulton — 810, Bowes — 910, Wilson — 1,928. The election of Wilson as Mayor reflected the deep suspicion of the inhabitants that they had been taken advantage of by railway interests. At the same time it demonstrated that the city would no longer comply blindly with requests of railway men — Wilson summed up this new philosophy of railways in remarks upon the Esplanade project:

> In whatever way this subject is considered it is the most disastrous project for all parties but the speculators, jobbers and railway contractors and companies, which was ever conceived, and the greatest calamity which has even fallen upon the City. It was commenced badly, it was conducted disgracefully, and it has ended disastrously. If it be possible to

take a lesson from the past — when railway jobbers want a road constructed let them construct it themselves as best they can at their own expense.

Wilson was easily re-elected Mayor in January 1860 and his popularity aided his election to the legislative assembly for York North that same month. Recognizing the advantages of having a representative of the corporation, in this case the Mayor himself, in an assembly where important railway interests were strongly represented, council enthusiastically granted Wilson a leave of absence to travel to Quebec to attend the sessions.

One event Wilson could not miss was the impending visit to Toronto of the Prince of Wales. Months of elaborate planning went into Toronto's first Royal Visit and council authorized expenditures of some $12,000 for elaborate decorations, such as the traditional arches and gala civic receptions. Aside from some embarrassment caused by the Orange Order's refusal to disengage itself from the festivities, even after a special request by Mayor Wilson, the Prince's visit was a spectacular success. Arriving in Toronto on September 7th 1860, on the steamer *Kingston*, the Prince was received on the dock by all of the city's luminaries, including Mayor Wilson, as well as thousands of spectators who sang God Save the Queen. Official functions which followed included a reception at Osgoode Hall, a review of the troops at Queen's Park, a visit to the University of Toronto and, of course, the traditional ball where the Prince reportedly danced till four in the morning.

Wilson did not seek a third term as Mayor, preferring to turn his full attention to provincial matters. In May 1862 he became a member of the executive council and solicitor-general in the administration of John Sandfield Macdonald and Louis-Victor Sicotte. A Year later he left politics altogether when he was elevated to the bench, serving first as puisne judge of the Court of Queen's Bench, then as judge in the Court of Common Pleas. In 1868 he returned to Queen's Bench. In 1871 he was appointed a member of the Law Reform Commission and in 1878 he was made chief justice of the Court of Common Pleas. In 1884 Wilson was made chief justice of the Court of Queen's Bench.

Adam Wilson retired from the bench in 1887. That same year he accepted a Knight Bachelor from Queen Victoria, an honour he had apparently refused earlier. For his remaining years Sir Adam, one of Toronto's most distinguished citizens, quietly divided his time between his home on Spadina Crescent and his Balmy Beach cottage.

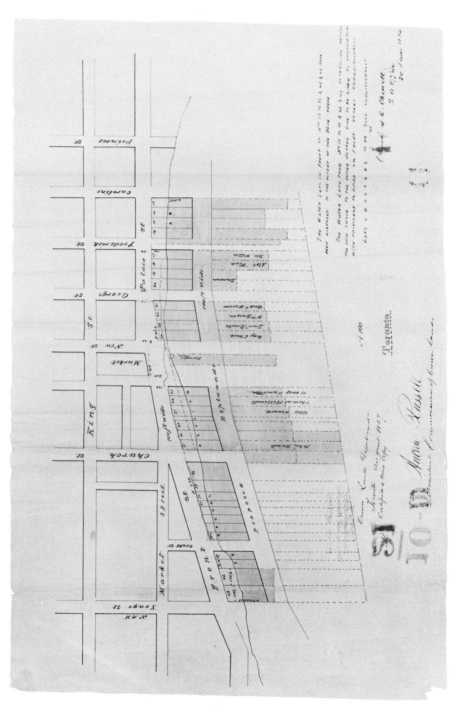

75

FRANCIS HENRY MEDCALF, foundry owner and politician; b. 10 May 1803 in Ireland; d. 26 March 1880 in Toronto.

FRANCIS HENRY MEDCALF
MAYOR 1864-66, 1874-75

The sixteenth man to fill the mayor's chair was Francis Henry Medcalf. First elected to council in 1860 as alderman for St Lawrence Ward, he sat on council again in 1863 as alderman for St David's Ward. In December 1863 he was nominated for Mayor and in the ensuing January election defeated the incumbent, John George Bowes (q.v.), by a vote of 2,276 to 2,114. In the 1865 mayoralty race, Medcalf turned aside a challenge from John Hillyard Cameron and the following year his public support was so strong that he was returned by acclamation. Firmly ensconced as the public choice, Medcalf must have seemed unbeatable at the polls. However, in 1867 the selection of the mayor was returned to the aldermen-elect, and although Medcalf could rally the support of the electors he could not win the support of his fellow aldermen. Consequently, in January 1867, after having been duly elected alderman for St David's Ward, Medcalf's name was turned down in council by a vote of 12 to 9.

Medcalf remained on council until the end of 1871, but was unable to gain the support of a majority of his fellow members of council. Then in March 1871 he unsuccessfully ran for parliament as a conservative in the east Riding of Toronto. Absent from politics in 1872 and 1873, he had his revenge in 1874 when the election of the Mayor was once again to be by popular vote, scoring an easy victory. In 1875 he easily won the mayoralty again, but by the end of

77

this, his last term, it was obvious to most that the elderly Medcalf was no longer the best choice. Undaunted, he stood for re-election in 1876 and, to everyone's surprise, again in 1877, only to lose both contests to the popular Angus Morrison (q.v.).

Much of Medcalf's support during his municipal career was undoubtedly the result of his involvement in the Orange Order. A staunch Conservative and ardent Protestant, he had served in many official capacities in the Orange lodges of Toronto: he was master of a local lodge, district master for Toronto from 1854-62, and from 1862 to 1864 (the first year he was elected Mayor) provincial grand master of Canada West.

F.H. Medcalf's public appeal was determined, however, not only by his fraternal affiliations but also by his image as an "honest, hardworking, self-made man." The son of Irish parents who had come to Upper Canada with a family of eight children in 1819, the enterprising Medcalf had gone to Philadelphia at the age of 20 and trained as a millwright and blacksmith. He returned to Toronto in 1839 and within a few years had opened the Don Foundry and Machine Shops specializing in farm machinery, steam engines, and heavy castings. The success of the Don Foundry, despite being burned out at least 5 times, earned Medcalf considerable respect and even more money. At the same time, his ability to exploit his "rags to riches" story, including the nickname "Old Squaretoes" (a reference to his work boots), did much to further his municipal career.

Medcalf's mayoralties, though almost a decade apart, were dominated by perennial municipal problems. Recurrent issues such as water supply, street repairs, crime control, relations with the railways, and taxes dominated the committee rooms and council chamber. Considering the bad luck Mayor Medcalf had experience with his own foundry, it is not surprising that the city council took steps in 1874 toward establishing a fire brigade with a permanent staff. Prior to this time only the chief and his officers were full-time employees, while the men of the company were volunteers who were paid a retainer if they responded to a fire alarm. The standing committee on fire, light and gas recommended the establishment of a permanent company of 36 men; the adoption of this recommendation was an important step in the development of the fire department as we know it today.

During his last year as Mayor, Medcalf was granted leave to attend a banquet sponsored by the Lord Mayor of London in honour of all the mayors in the Commonwealth. Medcalf travelled to England at his own expense, and in July 1875 appeared at Guildhall as the representative of Toronto. The affair was widely reported and it was said Medcalf cut a fine figure attired in a "dress suit, a robe or cloak of scarlet broadcloth, richly trimmed with Russian sable and black velvet and lined with white satin, and a black cocked hat."

Medcalf spent his last years in Toronto in relative quiet while his sons operated the business. When news of his death reached the council a motion of "deep sorrow" passed unanimously and his funeral produced an enormous parade of the city's fraternal regalia.

JAMES EDWARD SMITH, merchant and politician; b. 25 December 1831 in London, England; d. 9 March 1892 in Toronto.

JAMES EDWARD SMITH
MAYOR 1867-68

James Edward Smith was born in England and brought to Canada by his parents about 1841. After receiving "a first-rate education," he studied for some time in the law office of Henry Sherwood (q.v.) Young Smith did not however finish his legal training, and by the late 1850's he was proprietor of a wholesale grocery business in Brocton, a small incorporated village later annexed to Toronto. By 1861 James E. Smith & Co. had moved to Church Street,near Colborne, in the commercial heart of the city. Dealing in the importation of wholesale grocery products and wines and liquors, the company flourished, and this prosperity led to the inevitable investments in real estate. About the same time, Smith became the agent for Imperial Insurance, a move that would later secure him his fortune.

Smith first became involved in municipal politics at the age of 26, being elected a councilman in 1857 and 1858. Elected alderman in 1859, Smith retained this position until his retirement from council in 1870. From the beginning of his municipal career, he took an active part in the proceedings in council as well as in committee and by the early 1860s his business and financial acumen had led to his being elected chairman of the important and powerful committee on finance and assessment.

In 1867 the responsibility of electing the Mayor, after some years of popular elections, was again vested in the city council.

Francis Henry Medcalf (q.v.), was the obvious choice of the electorate, successful in the last three elections and unopposed the previous year. However, when the council met to choose its presiding officer in January 1867, Medcalf was rejected by a vote of 12 to 9. Five other candidates went down in similar fashion during this long and apparently riotous meeting of the "City Fathers." Finally, Smith was nominated and was successful by one vote, his own. The next day the newspapers reported that his name had been cleverly withheld until all his opponents had been proposed and defeated, and that he had known full well that the pivotal vote, said to have been cast by Samuel Bickerton Harman (q.v.), was "in the bag."

As Mayor, Smith proved to be a capable administrator and, apparently to some critics' surprise, a hard worker. 1867 and 1868 were prosperous years for Toronto, now a city of nearly 50,000. The now well-cooled railway boom had, to be sure, left its mark on the finances of the corporation, but the regular duties of the civic officials, both elected and appointed, were little different from those of officials in private corporations. Local works were carefully monitored and administered by committee and council to assure that each ward received its fair share.

The highlight of Smith's mayoralty had little to do with local business. The Confederation of British North America was on everyone's mind, and as July 1st approached Toronto took very seriously the roles it would play: first as the capital of the new province of Ontario and secondly as a major city in the envisioned transcontinental dominion. Celebrations were organized by a special committee of council and advertisements describing the proposed programme began appearing in June. Mayor Smith, as chief magistrate, was of course the presiding official and is reported to have handled his duties with much decorum and dignity. The celebrations themselves included a review of Her Majesty's troops, regular and volunteer, at Bathurst Street Common, the laying of the cornerstone of the Volunteer's Monument in Queen's Park, a balloon ascension in the afternoon, and an "instrumental Promenade Concert in the evening at Queen's Park accompanied by a grand display of fireworks and massive illumination of the grounds by Chinese latterns and the like."

Re-elected in 1868, Smith presided over a prosperous but

uneventful year, though the new dominion suffered a setback when, in the early hours of April 7th, the Honorable Thomas D'Arcy McGee was assassinated in Ottawa. As a token of respect the council passed a deep felt resolution of sympathy, then adjourned. On November 6th, 1868 Smith was appointed to the lucrative post of collector of customs for the port of Toronto. Consequently, he let it be known that he would not serve another term as Mayor. Though he did retain his seat as alderman until 1870, Smith played only a minor role in proceedings of council and seems to have concentrated on his business interests and his new post. He continued to act as collector until November 19th 1879, when a public controversy led to his resignation.

Smith's business was styled J.E. and A. W. Smith after his son Alfred W. joined the firm. His earlier involvement in the fledgling insurance business began paying dividends, and the tremendous growth in insurance investments of the late 19th century made Smith a wealthy man. Although he left most of the business chores to his son, who by the 1890s was president of the Toronto Board of Underwriters, the elder Smith maintained an interest in the company's affairs. Smith passed away at his elegant house, Wellesley Hall, leaving an estate modestly estimated at $175,000. His funeral was attended by Toronto's leading citizens, including, of course, the Mayor and council. The honorary pallbearers included the Honorable John Beverley Robinson (q.v.), lieutenant governor and A.R. Boswell (q.v.), Smith's old ally on City Council.

SAMUEL BICKERTON HARMAN, lawyer, politician and civil servant; b. 20 December 1819 the son of Honorable Samuel Harman, Chief Baron of the Court of the Exchequer, British West Indies; d. 26 March 1892 in Toronto.

SAMUEL BICKERTON HARMAN
MAYOR 1869-70

Samuel Bickerton Harman succeeded James E. Smith (q.v.) on January 18th, 1869, to become Toronto's 18th Mayor. Born in England, Harman spent his youth in the West Indies where his father, the Honorable Samuel Harman, served as chief baron of the Court of the Exchequer. Young Harman was educated in England before returning to the West Indies in 1840 to begin his career with the Colonial Bank. He served as a clerk in Barbados and later as the bank's accountant and manager in Grenada.

After coming to Canada in 1848 to see to family investments, Harman decided to remain. Shortly after his arrival he began to study law and in 1855 was called to the bar of Upper Canada. Soon after he established his law practice, Harman's well-known acquaintance with accounting procedures led to his specialization in legal-financial transactions, and he was often selected to handle intricate arbitrations.

In 1866 he began his municipal career as alderman for St Andrew's Ward. He held this seat on council through 1872 and served as chairman of the finance committee. Upon the retirement of Mayor Smith in 1868, Harman, a close political ally of Smith's was elected Mayor by the council. Like Smith, Harman brought much-needed corporate-financial expertise to council dealings. At the same time, his legal training was considered invaluable and he served as chairman of a commission which produced the first complete consolidation of the city's by-laws.

Following his second term as Mayor, Harman remained on council but played on a minor role. In late 1872 he resigned from council to become the city's first assessment commissioner, charged with establishing a completely new department. In 1874, following the retirement of Andrew Taylor McCord, city treasurer for more than 38 years, Harman applied for and won the job of city treasurer and keeper of the seal. His interest in financial matters led to his being instrumental in obtaining a charter for the Institute of Chartered Accountants, and he served as this organization's president. He was an active member of the Corporation of Trinity College University, being awarded a DCL in 1878, and was one of the founders and members of the Council for the Canadian Institute. A Mason and an active member of the Church of England, who served a term as chancellor of the diocese, Harman was also interested in local history and genealogy, and was an honorary member of the New England Historical and Genealogical Society.

Harman served as city treasurer until November 1888, when poor health forced him to retire. In recognition of his more than 20 years of civic service City Council voted him a pension of $2,000 per annum, which he continued to receive until his death in 1892.

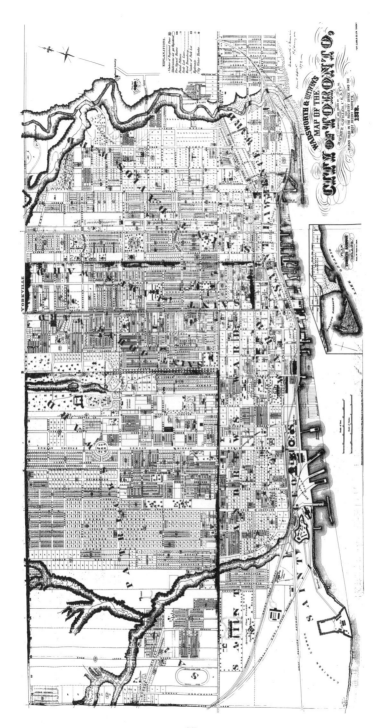

JOSEPH SHEARD, builder, architect and politician; b. 1813 in England, was the father of Dr Charles Sheard and the Honorable Matthew Sheard; d. 30 August 1883 in Toronto.

JOSEPH SHEARD
MAYOR 1871-72

The nineteenth man to serve as Mayor was Joseph Sheard, the unanimous choice of council at its meeting on January 16th 1871. Sheard, a well-known builder and contractor, had begun his municipal career some 20 years earlier, serving as alderman for St Patrick's Ward in 1851 and 1852. He sat on council in 1854-55, 1859, and again from 1866-76.

Sheard's election as Mayor was less a recognition of any executive ability than a reflection of the growing custom of electing men who had sat on council for many years. This prctice demonstrates not only the relative stability of the times but also the fact that most of the day-to-day work of the corporation was being done by the standing committees and the ever increasing civic service. To no one's surprise, Sheard's first term as Mayor was a quiet one. As was also becoming customary, he was unopposed in 1872 and served another uneventful term. He remained on council for four more aldermanic terms following his mayoralty. Upon his death in 1881, city council recognized his many years of service by passing a resolution to "the memory of one who has so faithfully served his fellow citizens as Mayor and Alderman, and from his long residence had become one of the landmarks of Toronto." Today the site on McGill Street of his residence is a City parkette bearing his name.

Joseph Sheard had come to Upper Canada in the 1830s. Born in

89

Yorkshire, England, the son of an officer in the Dublin Dragoons, he obviously had little formal education, for was forced to become an apprentice wheelwright and joiner upon the death of his father. By 1833 young Sheard had saved enough to pay his passage to America and, packing his tools, he sailed from Hull on April 15th aboard the "Foster." Landing at Quebec, he made his way by "Durham Boat" to Prescott, Upper Canada, where he boarded the steamer "William the Fourth" bound for York. The new arrival took up residence in what was known as "Macaulay Town," an area of working-class homes situated near the present City Hall at Bay and Queen streets. Finding his carpentry skills much in demand, he was soon able to buy a lot on McGill Street where he lived the rest of his life, a local fixture.

Joseph Sheard gained the respect and admiration of many Torontonians following the rebellion of 1837, when he refused to oversee the construction of the gallows to hang the condemned rebels, Samuel Lount and Peter Mathews. By the 1840's he was one of the most sought-after building contractors and, after going into business for himself, took on more responsibility for design as well as construction. He eventually assumed the title of "architect" and accepted such important commissions as the Ontario Bank building on the northeast corner of Scott and Wellington. His most impressive achievement, however, was certainly Cawthra House on the northeast corner of King and Bay.

Cawthra House has been described as "without doubt the finest and most elegant town house built in Toronto." Assisted by his partner and son-in-law, William Irving, Sheard began work on this magnificent structure in 1851. Two years later the Cawthra family moved in, remaining its occupants until 1884. The house was then occupied by a series of banks: the Molson Bank, the Sterling Bank, and finally the Bank of Nova Scotia. Attempts to save the house from demolition were unsuccessful, and in 1946 the landmark of Sheard's career was destroyed.

William Cawthra House, north-east corner of King and Bay Streets. Built in 1851 by architect (Mayor) Joseph Sheard, the house was demolished in 1946.

ALEXANDER MANNING, builder, architect and politician; b. 11 May 1819 in Ireland; d. 20 October 1903 in Toronto.

ALEXANDER MANNING
MAYOR 1873, 1885

Alexander Manning, Toronto's twentieth Mayor, was the epitome of the self-made man. Born in Dublin, he came to Toronto in 1834 and, after a brief two year sojourn in Ohio returned as a building contractor. In a city that more than doubled its size in the decade after 1834, Manning earned many lucrative contracts. By the 1850s he was involved in the construction of numerous public buildings such as the Normal School (1853) and, most impressively, the Parliamentary Library in Ottawa in the 1860s. Predictably, Manning became involved in the lucrative construction contracts of the railway boom of the 1850s, both in Canada and in the United States.

The large profits earned by Manning were in turn reinvested by this astute businessman into such ventures as Traders Bank, the North America Land Company and the Toronto Brewing and Malting Company. However, Manning's main interest was in real estate and, aside from his huge private holdings he owned the Manning Arcade, the Grand Opera House and the Manning Chambers. By the time of his death in 1903, it was publicly recognized that Alexander Manning was the "largest individual ratepayer in Toronto."

Although he was reported to have declined nominations to run for parliament, Manning did not hesitate to become involved in municipal politics. He represented St Lawrence Ward on council in 1856 and 1857, and from 1867 to 1873, being chosen Mayor by council in the last year. It was during this term that he spearheaded the movement that led to the establishment of the Home for Incurables, a movement in which he would remain involved for many years.

In 1874 The mayor was again to be elected by a vote of the ratepayers, and Manning gave way to the popular Francis Henry Medcalf (q.v.), declaring himself retired from municipal politics. In 1881 Manning was again suggested as a candidate for Mayor but stood aside in favour of alderman Patrick G. Close, who in turn went down to defeat. Four years later Manning accepted the nomination of the local Tory machine and defeated the independent candidate, alderman John J. Withrow. Withrow had been an alderman for many years and many believed he should not have been challenged.

In his inaugural address Mayor Manning displayed the necessary concern with the local problems which plagued the city: the increasing filth of the streets, the foul state of the water supply and the ever-present concern with the city's finances and tax rate. These problems were not, however, easily or readily solved in one brief term, and Manning fully expected to be elected for a second term — unchallenged. This was not to be. Manning's challenge of Withrow, as well as the growing support of the civic reformers, produced much opposition and more importantly a candidate, William Holmes Howland (q.v.).

The 1886 election represented a first for most young Torontonians. It had been a long time since the candidates for Mayor had represented opposing political factions and had waged such a hard-fought campaign. Manning was assailed for his anti-temperance stand and electors were reminded that Manning owned large shares in a Toronto brewery. When the polls closed on Monday, January 4th 1886 Manning had been soundly defeated.

Manning was never again involved in politics, though he remained a well-known and popular public figure until his death in 1903.

Manning Arcade. One of the many properties developed by Alexander Manning, the Arcade on King St. West, was designed by the architect of City Hall (Queen St.) E.J. Lennox, and built in 1884.

ANGUS MORRISON, lawyer and politician; b. 20 January 1822 in Scotland, the son of Hugh and Mary Morrison (*née* Curan), and brother of Honorable Joseph Curan Morrison; d. 10 June 1882 in Toronto.

ANGUS MORRISON
MAYOR 1876-78

Angus Morrison, Toronto's twenty-first Mayor, was brought to Upper Canada by his father, a widower and retired "sergeant in the 42nd Royal Highland Regiment of Foot." Hugh Morrison settled in Georgina Township in June 1830, with the apparent intention of farming. By January 1831, however, he had married Fanny Montgomery, sister of John Montgomery of 1837 rebellion fame, and opened the Golden Ball Tavern.

In 1839 Angus joined the law firm of his brother Joseph as a clerk. Angus, an extremely popular and well-known young man in the city, was called to the bar in 1845 and set up his own law practice. Broad-chested and of average height, with thick curly hair and stylish mutton-shop sideburns, he was a gentleman of fashion. Much of his reputation, however, was based on his athletic achievements. In 1840 and 1841 he was declared "Champion of Toronto Bay" after winning the annual scull races on the lake, and as an avid curler he took part in many of the day-long matches held on the bay. Morrison aided in the organization of the Toronto Curling Club and the Toronto Rowing Club, serving as president of the latter for many years.

Predictably, Morrison parlayed his social position and public image into a substantial legal career and used them in 1853 to win public office, being elected alderman for St James's Ward. He then launched a long career in provincial politics, being elected member for North Simcoe, from 1854 to 1863, and for Niagara for 1864-74. In 1874 he attempted to win his home riding of Toronto Centre but was unsuccessful in a close riotous race. Morrison, who had held public office since 1853 with the exception of a few months in 1863-64, was now politically unemployed. In December 1874 he let his name be placed on the mayoralty ballot in Toronto, along with Francis Henry Medcalf (q.v.) and Andrew Taylor McCord, but withdrew from the contest before the poll. In the following December he actively pursued the nomination for Mayor and after a vigorous campaign easily defeated the incumbent, Medcalf. The Globe reported that Morrison's "personal popularity" was the key to his victory; indeed losing only one of the nine ward polls, he received 4,425 votes to Medcalf's 1,673.

As Mayor, Morrison characteristically maintained a high profile, using his office to reinforce his ever-increasing popularity. In 1876 he represented Toronto at the Centennial International Exhibition in Philadelphia, where he purchased a prize-winning fountain and donated it to the citizens of Toronto. At the same exhibition, he watched Ned Hanlan win the scull race and presented him with a gold watch. Easily re-elected in 1877 and 1878, Morrison proved a capable civic administrator. He completed a long-overdue reorganization of the Water Works Commission. In 1877 he concluded negotiations in Ottawa with the federal government which allowed the city to take over the garrison reserve to the west of the city as the permanent home of the exhibition (now the Canadian National Exhibition).

As during his first experience on council, Morrison found that railways were again an important issue for the corporation. The council had awarded $710,000 in bonuses to several railway projects, including $100,000 in 1873 to George Laidlaw's Credit Valley Railway. By the beginning of Morrison's first mayoral term, however, many of these railway schemes were in financial difficulty, especially in the Credit Valley. Morrison, a director and shareholder of the company as well as its solicitor, had been regarded by the promoters of the railway as a good choice for mayor, though some had expressed concern that he lacked the "vim" to push a second bonus through council. On March 7th, 1877, at a boisterous meeting of council replete with resignations, the bonus by-law for the Credit Valley was passed by a vote of 15 to

8. Bonus by-laws were subject to the approval of the ratepayers, a requirement of provincial law and Morrison chaired a public meeting to promote acceptance of the by-law. When the vote was taken on April 3rd, it was readily approved.

Nominated for the fourth term in December 1878, Morrison declined. Although he made at least one attempt to obtain an appointment from his political allies and would attempt a brief comeback in the mayoralty race for 1880, he appears to have retired from public life. His law firm, by this time styled Morrison, Sampson and Gordon, had flourished and undoubtedly provided him with a more than-adequate income. Morrison died unexpectedly during the night of June 10th at his substantial residence. He was an extremely popular figure, and his death was a shock to the entire community. His funeral, reported to have consisted of more than 90 carriages, was a civic event.

JAMES BEATY Jr, lawyer and politician; b. 10 November 1831 in Halton (Ontario), the son of John and Elizabeth Beaty (*née* Stewart), and nephew of James Beaty, newspaper man; d. 15 March 1899 in Toronto.

JAMES BEATY JR
MAYOR 1879-80

James Beaty Jr was Toronto's twenty-second mayor. Born on the family farm in Halton County, Beaty moved to Toronto to study law in the offices of Adam Wilson (q.v.) and Larratt Smith. Called to the bar in 1855, he became a partner in the firm the following year. An extraordinary lawyer, Beaty won the respect of the entire profession, earning a QC in 1872 and a DCL from Trinity College in 1875.

Beaty entered the political arena in 1877 as alderman for St James's Ward. He made his mark immediately by drafting By-law #793. Known as the "Beaty By-law," this act consolidated the ten existing standing committees into five and, more important, established the executive committee. From 1834 to 1877 the standing committee on finance and assessment virtually performed as the executive. Its status was evident from the fact that it met once a week while other standing committees, with the exception of the board of works, met only once a month. The "Beaty By-Law," however, clearly established this standing committee's pre-eminence by renaming it the executive committee and by giving it both control over every aspect of the corporation's activities and the authority to veto any expenditure.

Beaty had made his mark in municipal politics as a civic reformer, and in 1878, promising lower taxes, he ran for its top job. He could not, however, defeat the ever popular incumbent, Angus

Morrison (q.v.). In 1879 Morrison retired and Beaty ran again in the six-contestant race. Despite the candidacy of a well-known alderman, Patrick G. Close, and two ex-mayors, Alexander Manning (q.v.) and the indefatigable Francis Henry Medcalf (q.v.) Beaty won the race by 638 votes. He easily withstood a comback attempt from Angus Morrison in 1880 to win his second term.

Although Beaty ran his mayoralties with much efficiency and energy, he was by the middle of his second term looking to federal politics, presenting himself as a candidate in a by-election for West Toronto Riding. Turning his attention to the house of commons, where he was a supporter of Sir John A. Macdonald, Beaty did not run for Mayor in 1881. Credited with numerous "prominent acts of legislation," he was easily re-elected in the 1882 federal general election.

Upon his retirement from politics, Beaty spent much of his time writing and contributed numerous articles on politics and religion to journals, periodicals, and newspapers. Although it was never completed, he began a full-scale study of the origin of constitutional law in Canada. His one major work, *"Paying the paster: unscriptural and traditional"* reportedly created much discussion.

Beaty attempted a comeback in municipal politics in 1892, only to be humiliated at the polls. Beaty however never lost interest in local affairs and in 1895 he wrote a lengthy pamphlet entitled "Civic Relief," which included comprehensive proposals for civic reform.

James Beaty Jr died four years later at the residence of his son-in-law, A. J. Russell Snow, and was buried in the Necropolis.

Committee Room, City Hall (Front Street), c.1890.

WILLIAM BARCLAY MCMURRICH, lawyer and politician; b. 1 November 1842 in Toronto, the son of the Honorable John McMurrich; d. 6 September 1908 in Toronto.

WILLIAM BARCLAY McMURRICH
MAYOR 1881-82

William Barclay McMurrich, the eldest son of the Honorable John McMurrich, was born in 1842. Young McMurrich attended Upper Canada College and the University of Toronto, graduating as BA in 1863 and MA the next year. Though inclined towards the natural sciences (he won the Gold Medal at U of T in 1863), he chose to study law. Called to the bar in 1866, he soon established himself in his chosen profession.

McMurrich first entered civic politics in 1868, being elected school trustee for St Andrew's ward. As school trustee, the scholarly McMurrich used his considerable influence to support the development of free schools. He also served as chairman of the sites and building committee and visited the United States to investigate industrial schools; his report to the board was accepted and led to the founding of Toronto's first industrial school in the old House of Refuge building. Upon resigning from the board in 1877, McMurrich acted as the board's solicitor for the more than 30 years.

In 1879 and 1880 McMurrich won the aldermanic honours for St Patrick's Ward. He was chairman of the powerful executive committee that developed the local improvement system and, as he had also done for the board of education, McMurrich travelled to the U.S. in 1880 visiting cities where such a system was in vogue. The following year he ran for the mayoralty against alderman

Patrick G. Close, winning by a comfortable margin. During his mayoralty, McMurrich focused his legal training on administrative problems. During his first term he personally drew up a manual of the city, consolidating a number of the more important by-laws and their amendments. Re-elected in 1882, he inaugurated a system of contractor's deposits to protect the city against poorly completed or unfulfilled contracts. McMurrich retired from civic politics following his second term to contest the federal election in West Toronto. Running against former Mayor James Beaty (q.v.), he lost by less than 500 votes, a result duplicated five years later when he ran for Muskoka.

McMurrich had many interests, including the military. He had joined the Queen's Own Rifles in 1861 during the *Trent* affair and was later a member of the Victoria Rifles for 3 years. Twenty years after attending military schools in Toronto and Laprairie in 1864, he was gazetted captain of the Toronto Garrison Battery of Artillery. During the Northwest Rebellion of 1885, he acted as commandant of the fort at Toronto. McMurrich was also much involved in the traditional Scottish activities in the community. A secretary and president of the St Andrews Society, he was also an active member of the Presbyterian Church, being an elder at Knox Church, superintendent of the Knox Church Sabbath school, and commissioner to the Presbyterian General Assembly. His other interests and involvements were numerous: he was curator of the Royal Canadian Institute, the donator of the McMurrich silver medal in Natural Sciences at U of T, and a trustee at Upper Canada College, the Toronto Conservatory of Music, and the Prisoners' Aid Society. Business investments brought him directorships, with the Globe Company and the Boiler Inspection Company, and he was president of the Nipissing and James Bay Railway Company. A man involved in the early development of Muskoka, he was president and commodore of the Muskoka Lakes Association and, as already noted a candidate in the 1887 federal election for Muskoka.

McMurrich died in Muskoka in September 1908. His funeral was noted by a special meeting of council at which a suitable resolution was passed, and the council adjourned so that members could attend the funeral.

Mayor's Office, City Hall (Front Street), c.1899.

ARTHUR RADCLIFFE BOSWELL, lawyer, politician and yachtsman; b. 3 January 1838 in Cobourg (Ontario), the son of the Honorable George M. J. Boswell; d. 16 May 1925 in Toronto.

ARTHUR RADCLIFFE BOSWELL
MAYOR 1883-84

Arthur Radcliffe Boswell was born in Cobourg, Ontario on January 3rd 1838. His father, George Morse Jukes Boswell was one of Upper Canada's leading lawyers and claimed to be a descendant of the celebrated biographer of Doctor Samuel Johnson. Arthur was educated at Brockville and later Upper Canada College before studying law and being called to the bar in 1865.

Boswell entered civic politics in 1877 as alderman for St George's Ward, a seat he held until 1882 (with the exception of 1880). He served on several committees, including in 1882 as chairman of the executive committee. The next year he ran against John J. Withrow and in one of the closes mayoralty races in Toronto's history managed a 5 vote victory — 4,289 to 4,284. During Boswell's first term, the annexation of the village of Yorkville was completed, the first of many such annexations. He was re-elected by acclamation in 1884; Withrow, although nominated, declined to stand, giving way to the two term custom.

Boswell's second term (1884) coincided with the 50th anniversary of the city's incorporation. As early as 1882 preparations for the semi-centennial had been entrusted to a special committee of council consisting of the Mayor and nine aldermen. As the celebrations grew nearer a citizens' committee was also formed to aid in the planning of the festivities. The celebrations began on March 6th, the city's actual birthday, but most of the festivities took place during six days from 30 June to 5 July; each day was assigned a theme — municipal day, military day, trade and industry day, United Empire Loyalist day, benevolent societies' day, educational day — and included parades, historical tableaux, concerts, balls and athletic competitions, as well as evening fireworks and illuminations. The impressive programme was supplemented by the production of beautifully designed medals and by the publication by the city of a *Memorial volume*, a history of Toronto written by the eminent local historians, John Charles Dent and Dr Henry Scadding.

Involved in the preparations from the beginning, Boswell received a great deal of praise for his handling of the official duties, and during the public events was the epitome of the congenial host, attending all the events from early morning until late at night. Immaculate, yet robust and extremely enthusiastic, Mayor Boswell was the hit of the fair.

The popular Boswell did not choose to seek re-election in 1885 and returned to his legal practice, soon accepting appointments such as inspector of insurance and registrar of the Friendly Societies and Loan Company. However, for the next 40 years he continued to take an active and varied interest in the social life of the city. He was a Mason, a member of the Albany, York and Toronto Clubs, a trustee of the Toronto General Hospital, chairman of the Public Library Board, and also on the executive of the Ontario Fish and Game Protective Association.

Aside from political, business and social activities, the athletic Boswell achieved local notoriety for his involvement in his first love — boating. He served as president of the Canadian Association of Amateur Oarsmen. Regarded as one of the most expert yachtsmen on the lakes, for many years he was an active member of the Royal Canadian Yacht Club, and served as its commodore from 1879 to 1883 and again from 1889 to 1896. In 1907 he was made an honorary life member.

TORONTO CITY COUNCIL 1884.

J.A.CARROLL   W.MILLICHAMP   J.IRWIN   J.JONES   D.DEFOE   J.BLEVINS   N.C.LOVE
T.A.HASTINGS   F.C.DENNISON   C.L.DENNISON   T.ALLEN   T.HUNTER   E.W.BARTON   M.WOODS   H.PIPER
W.SHEPHARD   T.J.ELLIOTT   DR.J.MCCONNELL   D.WALKER   W.CARLYLE   J.HARVIE   J.MAUGHAN   JOHN JAMES   W.ADAMSON
J.E.MITCHELL   J.T.MOORE   G.B.SMITH   W.W.FARLEY   GEO.VERRALL   JAS.BRANDON   JAS.LOBB   N.STINER   J.SHAW   T.DAVIES
JAS.CROCKER   A.R.BOSWELL, MAYOR.   J.TURNER.

111

WILLIAM HOLMES HOWLAND, businessman and politician; b. 11 June 1844 at Lambton Mills (Ontario), the son of Sir William Pearce Howland, Lieutenant-Governor of Ontario, 1868-73; and brother of Oliver Aiken Howland, Mayor of Toronto, 1901-2; d. 12 December 1893 in Toronto.

WILLIAM HOLMES HOWLAND
MAYOR 1886-87

William Holmes Howland, Toronto's twenty-fifth Mayor, was born at Lambton Mills, Canada West, in 1844, the eldest son of Sir William Pearce Howland. His father, the head of a wealthy and influential family, had made his fortune in the grain trade on the outskirts of Toronto. In public life he had been influential enough to be considered one of the lesser fathers of confederation and to earn both a knighthood and the position of lieutenant-governor of Ontario for his part in the negotiations.

The younger Howland was educated at Upper Canada College and the Model Grammar School in Toronto, but rather than pursue professional training he became involved in the family business when still a teenager. Quickly earning a reputation as a capable and aggressive business manager, Howland soon struck out on his own. Before the age of 30 he was involved in numerous financial enterprises and was the head of two insurance companies. Continuing his meteoric rise in financial circles in Toronto, he was elected president of the Board of Trade in 1874-75.

Consistent with his social standing in the community Howland was involved in patronizing various charitable organizations in the city, and following a conversion to evangelical Christianity, he launched himself on a campaign of religious reformism that would be unmatched by his contemporaries. Armed with wealth, respect and an influential name, this ardent temperance advocate spent virtually all of his spare time and much of his personal fortune on such causes as the Toronto General Hospital, the Christian Missionary Union and the Mimico Industrial School for Boys. He also developed a reputation for his keen interest in improving the living conditions of the slum dwellers of the city.

In the fall of 1885 Howland aimed his reformist zeal at municipal politics. Although a member of the well known Canada First Movement, he had previously participated only sporadically in politics. It was, however, a natural move. The source of the problems to which Howland had ardently addressed himself — drunkenness, slum conditions, filthy streets, and foul water supply — was, he thought, poor civic administration. Amidst a ground-swell of moral and practical reform, Howland forces launched a move to requisition him for the mayoralty. The campaign was under way.

One group whose presence on the local political scene was quickly felt was the newly created bloc of female voters. In March 1884 the Ontario legislature had decreed that unmarried women and widows of voting age who owned or rented property assessed at over $400 should have the municipal franchise. Middle-class and small in numbers, this block of voters would be actively sought by future mayoralty candidates. In the 1886 election with Howland representing morality, religion, and zealous reform, few contemporary observers doubted their preference. Despite a hard-fought campaign by the incumbent, Alexander Manning (q.v.), Howland and moral reform were easy winners.

Howland's first term was, to say the least, beset with controversies, beginning with no less than his temporary unseating as Mayor. The problem stemmed from financial difficulties the Mayor had suffered prior to his election, which had caused him to transfer his assets into his wife's name. He did not, as a consequence, have the property qualifications to be Mayor. When this was made public he was forced to retire and allow another election. After judiciously transferring the appropriate property back to himself, he appeared at the nomination meeting held by City Clerk John Blevins and, although the opposition had threatened to challenge, no other candidate appeared. Howland was confirmed as Mayor. His mayoralties were not to be without further controversy: a coal-supply scandal broke, in which senior city officials were arrested for misappropriation of funds; the city was rocked by a street railway strike in which the city, or at least Howland, backed the strikers only to see three days of serious rioting quelled by the presence of the militia. Moreover, the temperance Mayor's attempt to restrict the granting of liquor licences was soundly defeated in council. Perhaps his one moral achievement was the appointment of Inspector David Archibald of the police department as a one-man morality squad to fight vice and prostitution. Howland was not, however, ready to step aside and arguing it would take more than one term to produce the sought-after reforms, he let it be known that he would seek a second term. Though opposition produced a good candidate in bank president David Blain, Howland readily won the day.

During his second term he was in much the same position. Regular business of council and large local service projects dominated the council agenda. Projects such as the Don Improvements Scheme, and construction of a new City Hall and Court House, waterworks improvements, and street paving were to occupy the council's time. There was little time for moral reform. Again only one significant advance was made: the passage of the "Fleming Bylaw", named for its author R. J. Fleming (q.v.), which reduced the number of liquor licences issued by council. By the end of 1887 Howland had had enough, and to everyone's surprise he announced his intention to retire from civic politics at the age of 43. In retrospect, his mayoralty was perhaps more important not for his attemps to reform the social and moral conditions of the working class but rather for his basing his campaign on a specific programme. He had not served on city council before his election as Mayor, and he came to the council chamber not just to chair meetings and sign resolutions but also to participate and lead the council in directions he had proclaimed on the hustings.

Howland spent the years following his retirement from the mayoralty trying to sort out his personal business affairs. His fortune had suffered greatly from neglect and he was never able to recoup his losses. Moreover, his health deteriorated quickly and at the age of 49 he succumbed to an attack of pneumonia.

EDWARD FREDERICK CLARKE, editor, publisher and politician; b. 24 April 1850 in Ireland, the son of Richard and Ellen Clarke (*née* Reynolds); d. 3 March 1905 in Toronto.

EDWARD FREDERICK CLARKE
MAYOR 1888-91

Edward F. Clarke was born in Bailieboro, County Cavan, Ireland on April 24th 1850. Coming to Canada in the 1860s, "Ned" Clarke apprenticed as a printer as the *Globe* where, in 1872, he helped organize the notorious printers strike, an action which led to his being jailed briefly. By that time he had struck out on his own and founded the newspaper the *Orange Sentinel* which, as the voice of the Orange Order in Toronto, soon made Clarke a successful publisher, printer and, perhaps inevitably, an extremely successful Toronto politician. He was also later to serve in many executive positions in the Orange order, including deputy grand master.

Clarke entered mayoral politics in 1888 only a few short months after having won election as one of Toronto's representatives in the provincial legislature. As the Conservative-backed candidate, he hoped to capture the mayoralty from the Reformers, and when incumbent Mayor William Holmes Howland's (q. v.) surprise retirement was announced his chances looked good. When the candidates were finally settled upon at the ritual nomination meeting chaired by the city clerk, coal merchant Elias Rogers had taken Howland's place and the indefatigable Daniel Dafoe had entered the race. Nevertheless, the fight was between Clarke and Rogers.

Clarke brought to his 1888 campaign a political acumen almost unknown in civic politics up to that time. Although like his predecessor, Howland, he came to the mayoralty with no previous municipal experience, as a Conservative MPP for Toronto and an Orangeman he began the campaign with a large following. He cleverly cultivated women voters by employing female canvassers, he ingratiated himself with temperance advocates by declaring "he did not drink," and he easily swayed the growing labour vote by recalling his role in the 1872 printers strike. Open-minded civic reformers were enticed by his securing the endorsement of such notables as Goldwin Smith, who put his name in nomination. Clarke's popularity and his expert campaign foreshadowed doom for his opposition, but the death blow came at the height of the campaign when Clarke's friend and fellow Conservative MPP, N. Clark Wallace, made public proof of the existence of a local coal cartel involving none other than Clarke's adversary, Elias Rogers.

Clarke's stranglehold on elective office in Toronto was secure. He was unopposed in the 1889 election, and in 1890 he stood for and won a third term. In the next election Clarke's opponent was not taken seriously and the campaign attracted little attention. However, E.A. Macdonald captured a respectable portion of the vote, and for Clarke supporters the writing was on the wall. By the end of his fourth term, it was clear that he might not be able to win an unheard of fifth term. Opposition and criticism of his dual offices (he had continued to sit at Queen's Park) had mounted and, apparently against his will, Clarke retired from civic politics. With a touch of irony, the council voted to honour the retiring Clarke by presenting him with the mayor's chair — something he truly owned.

Clarke's achievements as Mayor were outstanding, especially considering that he had had no previous municipal experience. From the first council meeting, he took a very active role in the administration of civic affairs. He encouraged the adoption of modern business procedures, including new office machines, and reorganized and modernized the city treasurer's office following the retirement of Samuel Bickerton Harman (q.v.). The city solicitor's office was strengthened by enlarging the salaries of its officials, thereby allowing full time employment of more experienced and prestigious counsel. The city's finances, however, were the main target of his energies. He spent ever-increasing amounts on public works such as the Don Improvements, a new City Hall and court house, bridges, sewers and paving as the city's boundaries were extended by the annexation of five more suburbs. As these public works drew heavily on the city's finances, Clarke managed to negotiate the extension of credit with the provincial legislature, and in 1889 he and city treasurer were able to raise money in London, through the sale of city debentures.

His approach to the mayoralty was reflected in the civic reform recommendations of Alderman MacDougall. Feeling that better civic government must be based on a strong Mayor, at one point they even recommended that veto powers should be granted to the Mayor and suggested that a strong Mayor, would "have some chance to unify and regulate the civic policy of the year."

Following his retirement from the mayoralty, Clarke continued to sit as MPP for Toronto until 1894. Two years later he was elected to the federal parliament for West Toronto, a riding he held until his sudden illness and death in 1905. Clark's passing occasioned sincere regrets: upon hearing the news, the house of commons adjourned after panegyric speeches by Sir William Muloch and Sir Robert Borden. The funeral in Toronto was attended by so many that even a move to a larger church could not accommodate the throng.

ROBERT JOHN FLEMING, merchant and politician; b. 23 November 1854 in Toronto; d. 26 October 1925 in Toronto.

ROBERT JOHN FLEMING
MAYOR 1892-93, 1896-97

Robert John Fleming was born in Toronto on November 23rd, 1854, and was educated in local public schools. As a young entrepreneur of 24, Fleming was involved in the coal and wood business, operating his own storehouse on Parliament Street; but by 1884 he had abandoned the coal trade for the often more lucrative profession of real estate administration. During the next few years Fleming combined his considerable business skills with his no less considerable ambitions to achieve success in his chosen field.

R. J. Fleming's involvement in Toronto's real estate market, like many of his predecessors, inevitably led him to take an interest in civic affairs. An ardent temperance supporter, he joined the Howland crusade of 1886 and was swept into office as alderman for St David's Ward. Forceful and articulate, for three terms Fleming proved Howland's most important supporter, both in and out of the council chamber, and when Edward F. Clarke (q.v.) succeeded Howland, he became Clarke's most damaging critic.

Absent from council in 1890 and 1891, Fleming returned to civic politics in 1892 when, upon the retirement of Clarke, he sought mayoralty. Fleming's involvement in the next six mayoralty races (four of which he won) produced some of the hottest contests the city had ever seen; even the nationally oriented *Globe* moved civic election news from its traditional spot on page six to the front page.

Fleming's official opposition in the 1892 election was ex-mayor Clarke's choice, E. B. Osler, and ex-mayor James Beaty Jr. (q.v.), but the noisy contest was really between Fleming and Osler. On the hustings Fleming repeatedly struck out against the Clarke regime, promising a return to economic restraint and reduced taxes. As evidence of the need to "clean out the old gang at City Hall," he pointed to the fact that Osler, Clarke's hand-picked candidate, had left the city during the election — and that his campaign was in fact run by a committee of "familiar faces."

On election night huge crowds assembled at the respective headquarters of the candidates and by the end of the evening it was an easy victory for Fleming. In 1893 Fleming crushed the opposition candidate:

By the largest vote and greatest majority ever given a Mayoralty candidate in Toronto... they have endorsed the honest and economical administration of Mayor Fleming.

During his first two campaigns, Fleming became known as the "People's Bob," an image he took with him into office. As Mayor, he consistently refused to wear the silk top hat, white gloves and frocked coat that had become traditional attire for the Mayor during Council Meetings. Furthering his image of the hard-working, business-like official, painted lightly with a moral reformers brush, he brought to the Mayor's office a huge sign which he hung over his desk to remind everyone of his intentions:

Except the Lord keep the City
The Watchman waketh but in vain.

His two great successes (1892 and 1893) were not, surprisingly, enough to intimidate the opposition. In the 1894 mayoralty race, the "Ned Clarke" constituents put forward a strong candidate in the person of Warring Kennedy (q.v.). A close personal friend of Clarke and a man of recognized ability, he defeated Fleming by a sound margin. The following year Fleming was back in the race and turned the election into a hotly contested event once again. The campaign featured a candidates' meeting of some description almost every night: in the closest race since 1883 Kennedy held on to win, but only by 14 votes. When Kennedy declined to seek a third term in 1896, Fleming again came forward and this time was successful, easily defeating the capable John Shaw (q.v.). In 1897 the "People's Bob" had no difficulty retaining his office, soundly defeating long-time Alderman George McMurrich.

During his second two-year stint in office, one of the most significant administrative changes in the history of the city's government was instituted — the creation of the Board of Control. The increased demand for municipal services and the burden of administering these services put a great strain on the civic government. The Citizen's Reform Committee, chaired by such notables as Goldwin Smith, demanded a more business-like approach to civic government, with the creation of a small executive branch of government. The search for a new structure led to the creation of the Board of Control to handle daily all council business and to report to it for approval. Mayor Fleming presided over the board's first meeting on April 24th, 1896.

In August 1897 Fleming's municipal career took an interesting turn when, while still Mayor, he accepted the position of city assessment commissioner at a salary of $4,000 per annum. He resigned as Mayor, the council electing John Shaw to finish his 1897 term. A special committee of council was struck to prepare a resolution appreciative of his services and reported:

> That while suffering a loss in Mr. Fleming's retirement, the Council is pleased that his experience and talents will be used in the City's service...
> The committee further recommended that the Chair which Mr. Fleming has occupied as Mayor be presented to him as a memento of his terms of office.

The presentation was no doubt a reference to "Ned Clarke," who was the only other mayor granted such an honour.

Fleming continued to be assessment commissioner until 1903 when city commissioner Emerson Coatsworth died and the property department was amalgamated with the assessment department. Fleming thus became commissioner of property and assessment but left the civic service the next year to join the Toronto Railway Company of which he became general manager in

1905. He later played a significant role in the administration of various utility companies as general manager of the Toronto and Niagara Power Company, the Electrical Development Company, and the Toronto Electric Light Company. A director of the Toronto Board of Trade, he was a member of the Toronto Harbour Commission in 1921.

Fleming was not, however, finished with the mayoralty. In 1923, more than 25 years after last serving in that office, Fleming stood for election against Charles A. Maguire. More surprisingly, he came within 1,000 votes of election, polling 39,826 votes to Maguire's 40,815.

The "People's Bob" then retired to his estates in Pickering where he died suddenly on October 26th, 1925.

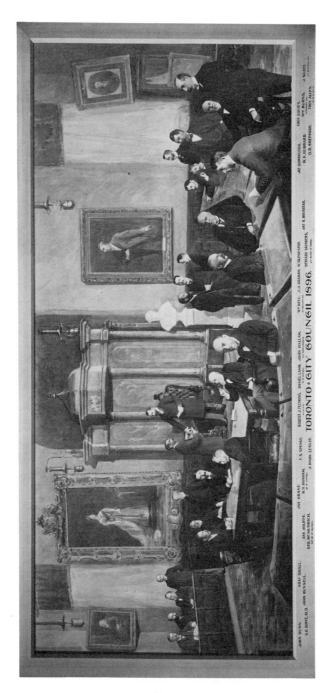

JOHN DUNN.   GEO. SMALL.   JAS. CRANE.   F. S. SPENCE.   ROBERT J. FLEMING.   DANIEL LAMB.   JOHN HALLAM.   WM. BELL.   J. J. GRAHAM.   W. T. STEWART.   TROY DAVIES.   J. SCOTT.
G.G. ROWE, M.D.   JOHN RUSSELL.   JAS. JOLLIFFE.   R. H. GRAHAM.   J. KNOX LESLIE.   JAS. GOWANLOCK.   W. P. HUBBARD.   BERNARD SAUNDERS.   JAS. B. BOUSTEAD.   WM. BURNS.   THOS. ALLEN.
                                 GEO. McMURRICH.   O. B. SHEPPARD.

TORONTO CITY COUNCIL 1896.

WARRING KENNEDY, merchant and politician; b. 1827 in Ireland; d. 25 June 1904 in Toronto.

WARRING KENNEDY
MAYOR 1894-95

Warring Kennedy was born in County Down, Ireland in 1827. After attending Grammar School in Londonderry, he was apprenticed in the dry good business in Kilrea, Ireland, later moving to Belfast. In 1857 Kennedy emigrated to Toronto where, because of his knowledge and experience of the dry good business, one of Toronto's leading industries in the 19th century, he had no difficulty finding suitable employment. Working for J. Macdonald and Company, he progressed rapidly in the trade, and within 10 years was reported to be in receipt of a salary of some $4,000 per annum.

In 1869, Kennedy entered into a partnership which established a new wholesale business styled, Samson, Kennedy and Gemmel (later, Samson, Kennedy and Co.). The success of the business was formidable, as the following description written in 1877 clearly demonstrates:

Messrs. Samson, Kennedy & Gemmel's warehouse is situated on the south-west corner of Scott and Colborne streets, one of the most central situations in Toronto. It is in the very heart of the business portion of the city, near the principal hotels, Custom House, and banks, and within a few minutes walk of the railway and steamboat depots. Some of the finest examples of street architecture to be found in the city are in

127

the immediate neighbourhood. Fronting on to Scott street are the magnificent buildings of the British America Insurance Company, the Pacific Block, the Bank of Ontario, the Montreal Telegraph Company, etc. Messrs. Samson, Kennedy and Gemmel's warehouse is a plain white brick structure of four storeys, (see plate 33) presenting no striking external features beyond its solidity and size. Internally it is one of the most complete, convenient, and commodious business houses in the city, affording four spacious and well lighted floors, each 50 by 123 feet, giving every facility for an effective display of goods. Passing through the various rooms a stranger is amazed at the immense piles and the variety of goods here displayed. On the basement floor are located unbleached cottons, flannels, blankets, unopened packages, etc. The ground floor contains an endless display of English and American bleached cottons, prints, and heavy goods. The third floor we find filled with an immense assortment of haberdashery, to enumerate which would require a respectable sized catalogue. Ribbons of all shades, widths and quantities are here, as are also laces of all kinds, to suit the taste of the millionaire or the humble cottager. The further floor exhibited a very large stock of black goods, fancy dress goods, muslins, parasols, shawls, silks, etc. This house was established in the fall of 1869, and by the enterprising management of the firm, not only partook of the general prosperity of the city, but attained a success that will compare favourably with the greatest commercial leaps that the last ten years have recorded. The system of management is that adopted by the large English houses, of placing each department under the control of an experienced manager. Mr. Samson, the senior partner, resides in Europe, and purchases all the heavy goods. Mr. Macaw, the junior partner, visits twice a year the English, French and German markets to purchase haberdashery and general fancy goods. A special buyer also visits periodically the Continental markets. The counting house is under the special control of Mr. Gemmel. The general management of the warehouse and the execution of all orders, are looked after by Mr. Kennedy.

As one of the City's most eminent businessmen, it was only natural that Kennedy take part in public life; but the unusually quiet and sedate Kennedy chose for the most part to become involved in many private associations rather than seek elective office. He was at various times President of the Commercial Travellers Association; Treasurer of the Commercial Traveller's Mutual Benefit Society; member of the Toronto Board of Trade; Director of the Yorkville and Toronto Christian Temperance Mission; President of Irish Protestant Benevolent Society; Senior Honorary Secretary and Treasurer of the Upper Canada Bible Society; and Chairman of the Board of Trustees of the Toronto General Burying Grounds Trust; a Methodist, Kennedy was secretary of the Toronto Conference and in June 1890 was a delegate to the Ecumenical Council held in Washington, D.C.

Prior to his nomination for Mayor in 1894, Kennedy had held only one brief elective public office; he had been alderman for St John's Ward in 1871. In 1877 he had stood for Mayor against the popular Angus Morrison (q.v.), but had been soundly defeated. But the choice of Kennedy by E. F. Clarke (q.v.) and his followers was a shrewd choice. For the city had fallen on hard times and the economic problems had caused much criticism of the incumbent administration of R. J. Fleming (q.v.). And who better to help in times like these than one of Toronto's, indeed Canada's, most successful business managers. The campaign that followed was low-key, as the distinguished, unabrasive Kennedy appeared in public, subdued but articulate, a man of "quiet authority." To the satisfaction of many, he defeated Fleming by a huge majority.

Mayor Kennedy stood for re-election in 1895 against another challenge from Fleming, and although the election was hotly contested between candidates, it received little public attention. In the lowest turnout in four years, Kennedy held on to beat Fleming by only 14 votes.

1895 was anything but a banner year for Mayor Kennedy. A civic investigation being carried out by County Court Judge MacDougall brought numerous reports of corruption and graft; and this, in turn, only added to the growing pressure to institute major admninistrative reforms. But, for Mayor Kennedy, the bottom really fell out in September of 1895, when his firm, Samson & Company, fell victim to the economic hard times and was forced into receivership, its stock being bought by the competition, the T. Eaton Company. Perforce, the Mayor had lost everything.

Kennedy retired from public life following his business collapse. During the next few years he was no doubt occupied sorting out his personal financial disaster; there is no evidence of how he managed except that from 1897 to 1899 he was an insurance agent for Mutual Reserve Fund Life Assurance of New York; and later he was Secretary-Treasurer of Toronto Orthopedic Hospital, a position which may have had some small remuneration. Upon his death in June 1904, the newspapers and the City Council briefly noted his death pointing out he had been one of the foremost and progressive businessmen of the City but had been retired from public life for some years.

City Council Chamber, City Hall (Front Street), c.1899.

JOHN SHAW, lawyer and politician; b. 1837 in Toronto, the son of George S. Shaw; d. 7 November 1917 in Toronto.

JOHN SHAW
MAYOR 1897-99

John Shaw was born in 1837, the son of George Shaw, a well-known and well-established builder in Toronto. Educated first at local public schools, John Shaw attended Upper Canada College, and later Victoria College, before studying law in the offices of the prestigious firm of Patterson and Harris. After being called to the bar in 1870, he established his own legal practice, before forming a partnership with John Blevins (later city clerk).

Although Shaw's business was downtown in the heart of the city on Toronto Street, he established his residence in the stylish family cottage in Yorkville on Bloor Street West. Upon the annexation of Yorkville to the City in 1883, Shaw was elected to represent the village (by this time St Paul's Ward) on city council. He remained an alderman for St Paul's Ward until 1891 when the ward boundaries were changed; he continued in council until 1895 as alderman for Ward 3. Shaw stood for Mayor in 1896 but was defeated by the strong incumbent R. J. Fleming (q.v.). Back in council as alderman for Ward 3 in 1897, Shaw was elected Mayor by the council to replace Fleming who had resigned to become assessment commissioner. Mayor Shaw was re-elected in 1898 and 1899, both times his opponent being E. A. Macdonald.

The single most important event of Mayor Shaw's terms of office was not based on politics or policies. It was the completion and occupation of the Queen Street City Hall. Designed by Toronto architect E. J. Lennox, construction was begun in 1889 and for ten years the citizens of Toronto had watched with interest the progress of this massive structure. By summer of 1898 the last stone went on and Mayor and Mrs Shaw and other civic officials braved a ride in a wooden workmen's lift to the top of the 240 foot clock tower. In September of 1899 the gala official ceremony took place. Shaw opened the door of the new municipal buildings with a gold key and made the following remarks:

> Why people will spend large sums of money on great buildings opens up a wider field of thought. It may, however, be roughly answered that great buildings symbolize a people's deeds and aspirations... It is now the most attractive place in Toronto, and will stand for generations to come, a splendid permanent mark and sign of the strong will, the energy and foresight, the splendid confidence and perfect faith of the citizens of Toronto in the future of their glorious city.

Mayor Shaw's faith in the future of the City seems to have had no constraints. Shaw was a forceful and energetic exponent of a "vision" which placed Toronto in the centre of a huge commercial empire, encompassing the entire province, especially the newly developing north. This "Northern vision" of the Mayor (and his many supporters) was in a very real sense, an identification of the need to capture the untold benefits of the development of Ontario's northland. "In order to maintain Toronto's position as a trading centre," Shaw argued, "Toronto's interests must be regarded as extending beyond civic boundaries."

To ensure that the City captured the products of the forests, farms, mines and lakes of the north, the Mayor dutifully presided over the establishment of the Toronto and Hudson's Bay Railway Commission, whose task it was to study the feasibility of building a railway from Toronto to Hudson's Bay. In June 1898 an expedition, financed by city council, was mounted and led by engineer W. T. Jennings. It set off to study the terrain first hand. Such enthusiasm was in evidence, that later that summer Shaw himself led a contingent of civic officials to be closer to the anticipated exciting results. Although Shaw's Toronto and Hudson's Bay Railway

Commission was not to produce the anticipated results — a railway — it, like the impressive City Hall, was a symbol of Toronto's confidence that it was on the verge of greatness. If the Prime Minister of Canada could assure the country that "the 20th century belonged to Canada" then the Mayor of Toronto was sure to add — "and most of it to Toronto.."

John Shaw left politics briefly following his mayoralty of 1899, but returned to council in 1904 and 1905 as a member of the board of control. Then, in 1908, he was elected to the provincial legislature as member for Toronto North but soon afterward retired from politics altogether. Shaw died in Toronto on November 7th, 1917.

CITY COUNCIL 1834 — 1899

THE CITY COUNCILS

1834
Mayor: William Lyon Mackenzie

Ward	Aldermen	Councilmen
St. Andrew	Thos. D. Morrison, M.D.	John Armstrong
	John Harper	John Doel
St. David	William Lyon Mackenzie	Franklin Jackes
	James Lesslie	Colin Drummond
St. George	Thomas Carfrae, Jr.	John Craig
	Edward Wright	George Gurnett
St. Lawrence	George Munro	William Arthurs
	George Duggan, Sr.	Lardner Bostwick
	Joseph Cawthra	Joshua G. Beard
St. Patrick	John E. Tims, M.D.	Joseph Turton
	Geo. T. Denison, Sr.	James Trotter

Mr. Duggan was unseated by judicial decision and Mr. Cawthra was elected in his place. Mr. Bostwick died in September and was succeeded by Mr. Beard. Dr. Rolph was originally elected for St. Patrick's Ward but refused to serve.

1835

Mayor: Robert Baldwin Sullivan

Ward	Aldermen	Councilmen
St. Andrew	T.D. Morrison, M.D.	John Doel
	John Harper	John Armstrong
		William Ketchum
St. David	Robt. B. Sullivan	Geo. Henderson
	Geo. Duggan, Sr.	Chas. Stotesbury
St. George	Thos. Carfrae, Jr.	John Craig
	Edward Wright	Alexander Rennie
	George Gurnett	
St. Lawrence	John King, M.D.	Joshua G. Beard
	Geo. Munro	Alex. Dixon
St. Patrick	Geo. T. Denison, Sr.	James Trotter
	Rich. H. Thornhill	Geo. Nichol

Mr. Armstrong resigned on June 5th and was succeeded by Mr. Ketchum.
Mr. Wright was unseated and Mr. Gurnett elected in his place, taking his seat on April 13th.

1836

Mayor: Thomas D. Morrison, M.D.

Ward	Aldermen	Councilmen
St. Andrew	Thos. D. Morrison. M.D.	John Doel
	John Harper	Wm. Ketchum
St. David	Jas. E. Small	Jas. Hervey Price
	James King	Edward McElderry
St. George	Geo. Gurnett	John Craig
	John King, M.D.	Geo. Walton
St. Lawrence	John Eastwood	James Beaty
	Wm. Cawthra	Wm. Arthurs
St. Patrick	Geo. T. Denison, Sr.	Thos. Cooper
	Rich. H. Thornhill	James Trotter

1837

Mayor: George Gurnett

Ward	Aldermen	Councilmen
St. Andrew	John Armstrong	John Ritchey
	John Powell	Hugh Carfrae
St. David	Simon E. Washburn	Geo. Henderson
	Chas. Stotesbury	James Turner
St. George	George Gurnett	John Craig
	John King, M.D.	Geo. Walton
St. Lawrence	Geo. Monro	Joshua G. Beard
	Alex. Dixon	James Browne
St. Patrick	Geo. T. Denison, Sr.	James Trotter
	Rich. H. Thornhill	Robert Blevins

1838

Mayor: John Powell

Ward	Aldermen	Councilmen
St. Andrew	John Powell	John Ritchey
	John Armstrong	Hugh Carfrae
St. David	Chas. Stotesbury	Geo. Henderson
	Jas. Newbigging	Alex. Hamilton
	Samuel E. Taylor	
	Geo. Duggan, Jr.	
St. George	James G. Chewett	Geo. Walton
	George Gurnett	John Craig
St. Lawrence	George Monro	Joshua G. Beard
	Alex. Dixon	James Browne
St. Patrick	Geo. T. Denison, Sr.	James Trotter
	Wm. H. Boulton	Robert Blevins

Mr. Newbigging died in February. His successor, Mr. Taylor, died in July, and Mr. Duggan was elected to the vacancy.

137

1839

Mayor: John Powell

Ward	Aldermen	Councilmen
St. Andrew	John Powell	Thos. Young
	John Armstrong	John Ritchey
St. David	Geo. Duggan, Jr.	Alex. Hamilton
	Chas. Stotesbury	Geo. Henderson
St. George	Geo. Gurnett	John Craig
	Jas. G. Chewett	Geo. Walton
St. Lawrence	Alex. Dixon	Robert Beard
	Geo. Monro	Joshua G. Beard
St. Patrick	Wm. H. Boulton	Wm. Mathers
	Geo. T. Denison, Sr.	Jas. Trotter

1840

Mayor: John Powell

Ward	Aldermen	Councilmen
St. Andrew	John Armstrong	John Ritchey
	John Powell	Thos. Young
St. David	Chas. Stotesbury	Geo. Henderson
		William Andrews
	Geo. Duggan, Jr.	Alex. Hamilton
St. George	John King, M.D.	Geo. Walton
	Geo. Gurnett	John Craig
St. Lawrence	Geo. Monro	Joshua G. Beard
	Alex. Dixon	Robert Beard
St. Patrick	Geo. T. Denison, Sr.	Jas. Trotter
	Wm. H. Boulton	Wm. Mathers

Mr. Henderson resigned in May and Mr. Andrews was elected in his stead.

1841

Mayor: George Monro

Ward	Aldermen	Councilmen
St. Andrew	John Powell	Richard Tinning
	Wm. B. Jarvis	
	John Armstrong	John Ritchey
St. David	Alex. Burnside, M.D.	Alex. Hamilton
	Chas. Stotesbury	Wm. Andrews
St. George	Geo. Gurnett	John Craig
	John King, M.D.	Geo. Walton
St. Lawrence	Alex. Dixon	Robert Beard
	Geo. Monro	Joshua G. Beard
St. Patrick	Wm. H. Boulton	Wm. Mathers
	Col. J.S. Macaulay	Robert Blevins
	Geo. T. Denison, Sr.	James Trotter

Mr. Powell resigned in September, Mr. Boulton in November, and Mr. Mathers in May, being succeeded by Mr. Jarvis, Col. Macaulay and Mr. Blevins, respectively.

1842

Mayor: Hon. Henry Sherwood

Ward	Aldermen	Councilmen
St. Andrew	John Armstrong	John Ritchey
	Wm. B. Jarvis	Richard Tinning
	Capt. J.M. Strachan	
St. David	Hon. H. Sherwood	Wm. Andrews
	Alex. Burnside, M.D.	Alex. Hamilton
St. George	John King, M.D.	Geo. Walton
	Geo. Gurnett	John Craig
St. Lawrence	Geo. Monro	Joshua G. Beard
	Alex. Dixon	Robert Beard
St. Patrick	Geo. T. Denison, Sr.	James Trotter
	Col. J.S. Macaulay	Robert Blevins
	Wm. H. Boulton	

Mr. Jarvis resigned in February; Col. Macaulay in January; and were succeeded by Capt. Strachan and Wm. H. Boulton respectively.

1843

Mayor: Hon. Henry Sherwood

Ward	Aldermen	Councilmen
St. Andrew	Geo. Duggan, Jr.	Richard Tinning
	John Armstrong	John Ritchey
St. David	Alex. Burnside, M.D.	Wm. A. Campbell
	Hon. H. Sherwood	Wm. Andrews
St. George	Geo. Gurnett	John Craig
	John King, M.D.	Geo. Walton
	Wm. Wakefield	
St. Lawrence	Alex. Dixon	Robert Beard
	Geo. Monro	Joshua G. Beard
St. Patrick	Geo. T. Denison, Sr.	Jonathan Dunn
	Geo. T. Denison, Jr.	James Trotter

Dr. King resigned in May and was succeeded by Mr. Wakefield. The Aldermen from St. Patrick's Ward were respectively the grandfather and the father of Lt. Col. Geo. T. Denison, retired Magistrate, of Heydon Villa.

1844

Mayor: Hon. Henry Sherwood

Ward	Aldermen	Councilmen
St. Andrew	John Armstrong	John Ritchey
	Geo. Duggan, Jr.	Richard Tinning
St. David	Hon. H. Sherwood	Sheldon Ward
	Alex. Burnside, M.D.	Wm. A. Campbell
St. George	Wm. Wakefield	Geo. Walton
	Geo. Gurnett	John Craig
St. Lawrence	Geo. Monro	Joshua G. Beard
	Alex. Dixon	Robert Beard
St. Patrick	Wm. H. Boulton	James Trotter
	Geo. T. Denison, Jr.	Jonathan Dunn

139

Mayor: William Henry Boulton

Ward	Aldermen	Councilmen
St. Andrew	Geo. Duggan, Jr.	Alex. Macdonald
	John Armstrong	John Ritchey
St. David	Angus Bethune	Samuel Mitchell
	Hon. H. Sherwood	Sheldon Ward
		George Platt
St. George	Geo. Gurnett	John Craig
	Wm. Wakefield	Geo. Walton
St. Lawrence	Robert Beard	Samuel Platt
	Geo. Monro	Joshua G. Beard
St. Patrick	Geo. T. Denison, Jr.	Jonathan Dunn
	Wm. H. Boulton	James Trotter

Mr. Ward died in July and was succeeded by Mr. Platt.

1846

Mayor: William Henry Boulton

Ward	Aldermen	Councilmen
St. Andrew	Hon. J.H. Cameron	John Ritchey
	Geo. Duggan, Jr.	Alex. Macdonald
St. David	Hon. H. Sherwood	Geo. Platt
	Angus Bethune	Samuel Mitchell
St. George	Wm. Wakefield	Thos. J. Preston
	Geo. Gurnett	John Craig
St. Lawrence	James Beaty	Joshua G. Beard
	Robert Beard	Samuel Platt
St. Patrick	Wm. H. Boulton	James Trotter
	Geo. T. Denison, Jr.	Jonathan Dunn

1847

Mayor: William Henry Boulton

Ward	Aldermen	Councilmen
St. Andrew	Geo. Duggan, Jr.	Samuel Shaw
	Hon. J.H. Cameron	John Ritchey
St. David	Joseph Workman, M.D.	William Davis
	Hon. H. Sherwood	George Platt
St. George	Geo. Gurnett	John Craig
	Wm. Wakefield	Thos. J. Preston
St. James	John Bell	Thos. Storm
	John Armstrong	Alex. Hamilton
St. Lawrence	J.H. Hagarty	Samuel Platt
	Robert Beard	
	James Beaty	Joshua G. Beard
St. Patrick	Geo. T. Denison, Jr.	John Carr
	Wm. H. Boulton	James Trotter

Mr. Hagarty resigned in May and Mr. Beard took his seat in August.

1848

Mayor: George Gurnett

Ward	Aldermen	Councilmen
St. Andrew	Geo. Percival Ridout	John Ritchey
	Geo. Duggan, Jr.	Samuel Shaw
		John Howcutt
St. David	Rich. Dempsey	Geo. Coulter
	Joseph Workman, M.D.	Wm. Davis
St. George	Wm. Wakefield	E.F. Whittemore
	Geo. Gurnett	John Craig
St. James	John Armstrong	Alex. Hamilton
	Hon. H. Sherwood	Edwin Bell
	John Bell	Thos. Storm
		Robert James, Jr.
St. Lawrence	James Beaty	John Smith
	Robert Beard	Samuel Platt
St. Patrick	Wm. A. Campbell	Robt. B. Denison
	Geo. T. Denison, Jr.	John Carr

Mr. Shaw resigned in April, Mr. Hamilton in May, Mr. Storm in March; Mr. Armstrong died in August.

1849

Mayor: George Gurnett

Ward	Aldermen	Councilmen
St. Andrew	Geo. Duggan, Jr.	Thos. Armstrong
	Geo. Percival Ridout	John Ritchey
St. David	Joseph Workman, M.D.	Wm. Davis
	Geo. W. Allan	Geo. Coulter
	Richard Dempsey	
St. George	Geo. Gurnett	John Craig
	Wm. Wakefield	James Ashfield
	Thos. Bell	E.F. Whittemore
		Samuel Thompson
St. James	John Bell	Robert James, Jr.
	Hon. H. Sherwood	Edwin Bell
St. Lawrence	Robert Beard	Samuel Platt
	James Beaty	John Smith
	Joshua G. Beard	John T. Smith
St. Patrick	Geo. T. Denison, Jr.	John Carr
	Wm. A. Campbell	Robert B. Denison

Mr. Craig, Mr. Wakefield, Mr. Smith and Mr. Whittemore resigned on April 16th; Mr. Beaty and Dr. Workman on July 9th.

141

Mayor: George Gurnett

Ward	Aldermen	Councilmen
St. Andrew	Geo. Duggan, Jr.	John Ritchey
		Thos. Armstrong
St. David	Rich. Dempsey	Wm. Davis
		Geo. Coulter
St. George	Geo. Gurnett	James Ashfield
		Samuel Thompson
St. James	John G. Bowes	Edwin Bell
		Robert James, Jr.
St. Lawrence	Joshua G. Beard	Samuel Platt
		John T. Smith
St. Patrick	Wm. A. Campbell	Jonathan Dunn
		John Bugg

(By legislation of 1849 only one alderman could be elected from each Ward).

1851

Mayor: John George Bowes

Ward	Aldermen	Councilmen
St. Andrew	Hon. J.H. Cameron	John Ritchey
	Geo. Percival Ridout	John Carr
St. David	Richard Kneeshaw	Adam Beatty
	Richard Dempsey	David C. Maclean
St. George	Geo. Gurnett	James Ashfield
	Wm. Wakefield	
	Samuel Thompson	Edward Wright
St. James	John G. Bowes	James Price
	E.F. Whittemore	Michael P. Hayes
St. Lawrence	Robert Beard	John T. Smith
	Joshua G. Beard	Samuel Platt
St. Patrick	John B. Robinson	Jonathan Dunn
	Joseph Sheard	John Bugg

(By the repeal of former legislation two aldermen from each Ward were again to be elected).
Mr. Geo. Gurnett resigned and was appointed Police Magistrate on Jan. 24th.

1852

Mayor: John George Bowes

Ward	Aldermen	Councilmen
St. Andrew	Hon. J.H. Cameron	John Carr
	Thos. Armstrong	Kivas Tully
St. David	Rich. Dempsey	Adam Beatty
	Geo. Brooke	Geo. Platt
St. George	Wm. Wakefield	Jas. Ashfield
	Capt. J.M. Strachan	
	Samuel Thompson	Edward Wright
St. James	John G. Bowes	Chas. E. Romain
	John Hutchison	R.C. McMullen

St. Lawrence	Robert Beard	John T. Smith
	Joshua G. Beard	Joseph Lee
St. Patrick	Wm. H. Boulton	Jonathan Dunn
	Joseph Sheard	John Bugg

Mr. Wakefield resigned in March.

1853

Mayor: John George Bowes

Ward	Aldermen	Councilmen
St. Andrew	Thos. Armstrong, John Carr	Alex. Macdonald
	Joseph Dixon, Samuel Shaw	Samuel Rogers
St. David	John Bell, James Beaty	George Platt
	Geo. Brooke, Samuel Platt	William Davis
St. George	Samuel Thompson	James Ashfield
	E.H. Rutherford	Edward Wright
		Fred. C. Capreol
St. James	John G. Bowes	Chas. E. Romain
	John Hutchison, Angus Morrison	Samuel T. Green
St. John	J.L. Robinson	John Bugg
	Ogle R. Gowan	Wm. Hall
		Robert Dodds
St. Lawrence	Michael P. Hayes	John Smith
	Wm. Gooderham	Thos. McConkey
		Joseph Lee
St. Patrick	Geo. T. Denison, Jr.	Jonathan Dunn
	John B. Robinson	John Baxter
	Hon. Wm. Cayley	

Messrs. Carr, Bell, Brooke, Hutchison, Denison, Wright, Bugg and Smith resigned on Nov. 3rd. Mr. Dixon's return was set aside by judicial decision.

1854

Mayor: Joshua George Beard

Ward	Aldermen	Councilmen
St. Andrew	John Carr	Wm. Graham
	Chas. March	E.B. Gilbert
St. David	Samuel Platt	Adam Beatty
	Geo. W. Allan	John Carruthers
St. George	John Duggan	S.H. Thompson
	E.H. Rutherford	Edward Wright
St. James	Chas. E. Romain	John T. Smith
	Angus Morrison	James Good
St. John	Ogle R. Gowan	John Bugg
	Hon. J.H. Cameron	Joseph Rowell
	Joseph Sheard	
St. Lawrence	Joshua G. Beard	Thos. McConkey
	Joseph Lee	Wm. Murphy
St. Patrick	John B. Robinson	Thos. Mara
	Jonathan Dunn	Theophilus Earl

President from Jan. to Apr. during the Mayor's illness John Beverley Robinson. Mr. Gowan was unseated by judicial decision.

143

1855

Mayor: George William Allan

Ward	Aldermen	Councilmen
St. Andrew	John Carr	E.B. Gilbert
	Robt. P. Crooks	Henry Prettie
St. David	Geo. W. Allan	Adam Beatty
	Wm. Henderson	John Carruthers
		Wm. Ramsay
St. George	John Duggan	Edward Wright
	Geo. A. Philpotts	Andrew Drummond
St. James	Chas. E. Romain	John Wilson
	James Good	Alex. M. Smith
St. John	Hon. J.H. Cameron	John Bugg
	Richard Dempsey	Robert Moodie
	Joseph Sheard	Joseph Rowell
St. Lawrence	John Smith	Wm. Murphy
	Wm. Gooderham	Thos. McConkey
St. Patrick	Jonathan Dunn	Thos. Mara
	A. Wilson	Theophilus Earl

Mr. Dempsey and Mr. Moodie were both unseated by judicial decision.

1856

Mayor: John Beverley Robinson

Ward	Aldermen	Coouncilmen
St. Andrew	John Worthington	Henry Prettie
	Robt. P. Crooks	Henry Sproatt
St. David	Wm. Henderson	Adam Beatty
	John G. Bowes	John Carruthers
St. George	John Duggan	Edward Wright
	Geo. A. Philpotts	Geo. Netting
St. James	John Harrington	John Wilson
	John Hutchison	John Cameron
St. John	John Bugg	Joseph Rowell
	Richard Demspey	Robt. Moodie
St. Lawrence	Alexander Manning	Wm. Davis
	Wm. Strachan	Wm. Murphy
St. Patrick	John B. Robinson	Thos. Shortis
	Jonathan Dunn	Theophilus Earl

1857

Mayor: John Hutchison

Ward	Aldermen	Councilmen
St. Andrew	John Worthington	Henry Prettie
	Robt. P. Crooks	Henry Sproatt
St. David	John O'Donoghoe	Wm. Ardagh
	John Ritchey, Jr.	Wm. Ramsay
St. George	Alfred Brunel	Edward Wright
	Geo. A. Philpotts	Geo. Netting
St. James	John Harrington	Thomas Craig
	John Hutchison	William Fox

St. John	Richard Dempsey	Robt. Moodie
	John Bugg	Jas. E. Smith
St. Lawrence	Oliver Mowat	Wm. Davis
		W.M. Gorrie
	Alex. Manning	Wm. Murphy
St. Patrick	John B. Robinson	Theophilus Earl
	Thos. Shortis	Geo. Simpson

Mr. Davis was unseated and Mr. Gorrie was his successor.

1858

Mayor: William Henry Boulton
(until Nov. 8th, when he resigned.)
David Breckenridge Read
(for the rest of the year)

Ward	Aldermen	Coucilmen
St. Andrew	Wm. H. Boulton	Henry Sproatt
	John Carr	Abel Wilcock
St. David	Jeremiah Carty	Wm. Ardagh
	John Ritchey, Jr.	John Carruthers
		Wm. Ramsay
St. George	Alfred Brunel	Chris. Mitchell
	George Boomer	Frederick Upton
St. James	Oliver Mowat	Wm. W. Fox
	Alex. M. Smith	Thos. Craig
St. John	John Bugg	Robt. J. Griffiths
	Robt. Moodie	Jas. E. Smith
St. Lawrence	Geo. Ewart	Wm. Lennox
	Wm. Strachan	W.M. Gorrie
St. Patrick	Jonathan Dunn	John Purdy
	David B. Read	Henry Prettie

1859

Mayor: Adam Wilson

Ward	Aldermen	Councilmen
St. Andrew	Henry Sproatt	Abel Wilcock
	Thos. McCleary	Erastus Wiman
St. David	Jeremiah Carty	Wm. Ardagh
	John O'Donoghoe	John Reed
St. George	Alfred Brunel	Wm. S. Finch
	Samuel Sherwood, Kivas Tully	John E. Pell
St. James	Joseph Sheard	John Sterling
	Wm. W. Fox	John W. Drummond
	Alex. M. Smith, M.C. Cameron	Robt. Mitchell
St. John	John Bugg	Robt. J. Griffith
	Jas. E. Smith	John Boxall
St. Lawrence	Geo. Ewart	Thos. Berkinshaw
	James Stock	Archibald Taylor
St. Patrick	Jonathan Dunn	Geo. Carroll
	Michael Lawlor, M.D.	Wm. A. Lee

Mr. Brunel, Mr. Sheard, Mr. Drummond and Mr. A.W. Smith resigned during the year.

Mayor: Adam Wilson

Ward	Aldermen	Councilmen
St. Andrew	Henry Sproatt	Patrick Conlin
	Henry Godson	Robert Bell
St. David	Jeremiah Carty	Wm. Ardagh
	James J. Vance	John Carruthers
St. George	Samuel Sherwood	Edmund L. Butters
	John McMurrich	John E. Pell
St. James	John Smith	Chas. E. Stotesbury
	Wm. W. Fox	David Smith
St. John	Robt. Moodie	Robt. J. Griffith
	Jas. E. Smith	Jas. Farrell
St. Lawrence	Geo. Ewart	Wm. Higgins
	Francis H. Medcalf	Archibald Taylor
	Wm. Strachan	
St. Patrick	Jonathan Dunn	John Baxter
	John Carr	Robt. McKnight

After Mr. Ewart resigned Mr. Medcalf was elected in his place.

1861

Mayor: John George Bowes

Ward	Aldermen	Councilmen
St. Andrew	Henry Godson	Robert Bell
	Henry Sproatt	Patrick Conlin
St. David	John Ritchey, Jr.	John Reed
	Thos. Snarr	James Spottiswood
St. George	Geo. Boomer	John E. Pell
	Alfred Brunel	Frederick Upton
		Samuel Sherwood
St. James	John Nasmith	Wm. Edwards
	John Sterling	Neil C. Love
St. John	Robt. Moodie	John Boxall
	James E. Smith	James Farrell
St. Lawrence	Wm. Strachan	Wm. Higgins
	James Stock	Thos. Thompson
St. Patrick	John Carr	John Baxter
	Jonathan Dunn	Robt. McKnight

Mr. Upton died during the year and was succeeded by Mr. Sherwood.

1862

Mayor: John George Bowes

Ward	Aldermen	Councilmen
St. Andrew	Henry Godson	Robert Bell
	Henry Sproatt	Patrick Conlin
St. David	Patrick Hynes	John Reed
	John Smith	James Spottiswood

Ward	Aldermen	Councilmen
St. George	Alfred Brunel	Thos. Smith
	Stephen M. Jarvis	Richard Tinning, Jr.
St. James	John Nasmith	Wm. Edwards
	John Sterling	Neil C. Love
St. John	Robt. Moodie	John Boxall
	James E. Smith	James Farrell
St. Lawrence	George Leslie	Wm. Higgins
	Wm. Strachan	Thos. Thompson
St. Patrick	John Carr	John Baxter
	Jonathan Dunn	Nathaniel Dickey

1863

Mayor: John George Bowes

Ward	Aldermen	Councilmen
St. Andrew	Henry Sproatt	Robert Bell
	John Wallis	John Spence
St. David	Patrick Hynes	James Kerr
	Francis H. Medcalf	James Mitchell
St. George	Stephen M. Jarvis	James Bennett
	Thos. Smith	Richard Tinning, Jr.
St. James	Neil C. Love	Wm. Edwards
	John Sterling	Robt. James, Jr.
St. John	Robt. Moodie	John Boxall
	James E. Smith	James Farrell
St. Lawrence	Geo. Ewart	John O'Connell
	Wm. Strachan	Thos. Thompson
St. Patrick	John Carr	John Baxter
	Jonathan Dunn	Nathaniel Dickey

1864

Mayor: Francis H. Medcalf

Ward	Aldermen	Councilmen
St. Andrew	Henry Godson	Robt. Bell
	John Wallis	John Spence
St. David	Patrick Hynes	Wm. Adamson
	James J. Vance	Richard Ardagh
St. George	Stephen M. Jarvis	James Bennett
	Thos. Smith	Richard Tinning, Jr.
St. James	Neil C. Love	Wm. Edwards
	John Sterling	Robt. James, Jr.
St. John	Robt. Moodie	James Farrell
	James E. Smith	John Greenlees
St. Lawrence	Geo. Ewart	John O'Connell
	Wm. Strachan	Thos. Thompson
St. Patrick	John Baxter	Nathaniel Dickey
	John Carr	John Canavan
	Nathanial Dickey	James R. Dunn

Mr. Carr resigned and was subsequently appointed City Clerk. Mr. Dickey, resigning as Councilman, was elected as Alderman in Mr. Carr's place, and Mr. Canavan was elected Councilman.

Mayor: Francis H. Medcalf

Ward	Aldermen	Councilmen
St. Andrew	Henry Godson	Robt. Bell
	John Wallis	John Spence
	Robt. P. Crooks	
St. David	Patrick Hynes	Wm. Adamson
	James J. Vance	Jas. B. Boustead
St. George	Thos. Smith	Richard Tinning, Jr.
	John J. Vickers	John Clements
St. John	James E. Smith	John Greenlees
	Robt. Moodie	John Boxall
	Robt. J. Griffith	
St. James	Jospeh Sheard	Geo. T. Beard
	Robt. James, Jr.	James Fraser
St. Lawrence	Wm. Strachan	James Burns
	Thos. Thompson	Wm. Hamilton, Jr.
St. Patrick	John Canavan	James R. Dunn
	Nathaniel Dickey	Geo. T. Denison, Jr.

Mr. Wallis resigned in the course of the year and Mr. Moodie died.

1866

Mayor: Francis H. Medcalf

Ward	Aldermen	Councilmen
St. Andrew	Samuel B. Harman	Robert Bell
	Geo. D'Arcy Boulton	John Spence
St. David	Wm. Adamson	John Carruthers
	Patrick Hynes	Samuel Parker
St. George	Thos. Smith	Richard Tinning, Jr.
	John J.Vickers	John Clements
St. James	Joseph Sheard	James B. Boustead
	Wm. Edwards	James Fraser
		Geo. T. Beard
St. John	James E. Smith	John Boxall
	John Greenlees	Francis Riddell
St. Lawrence	Wm. Strachan	James Burns
	Thos. Thompson	John O'Connell
St. Patrick	Nathaniel Dickey	Geo. T. Denison, Jr.
	John Baxter	James R. Dunn

1867

Mayor: James E. Smith

Aldermen

St. Andrew	Samuel B. Harman	Geo. D'Arcy Boulton	Robt. Bell
St. David	Patrick Hynes	Francis H. Medcalf	Wm. Adamson
St. George	John J. Vickers	Thos. Smith	James D. Edgar
			John Clements
St. James	Joseph Sheard	Geo. T. Beard	Geo. Ewart

St. John	John Boxall	Francis Riddell	James E. Smith
St. Lawrence	Alex. Manning	Thos. Thompson	Wm. Strachan
St. Patrick	Robt. A. Harrison	Nathaniel Dickey	Geo. T. Denison, Jr.

(The election of Mayor was again committed to the Council, the office of councilman was abolished and three aldermen were elected from each Ward to hold office for three years, retiring in rotation.)

1868

Mayor: James E. Smith

Aldermen

St. Andrew	Robert Bell	Samuel B. Harman	G. D'Arcy Boulton
St. David	John Boyd	Patrick Hynes	Francis H. Medcalf
	Wm. Adamson		
St. George	John Clements	John J. Vickers	Thos. Smith
St. James	Alex. Henderson	Joseph Sheard	Geo. T. Beard
St. John	James E. Smith	John Boxall	Francis Riddell
St. Lawrence	Wm. Strachan	Alex. Manning	Thos. Thompson
St. Patrick	John Baxter	Robt. A. Harrison	Nathaniel Dickey

Mr. Boyd was unseated by judicial decision and Mr. Adamson took his place.

1869

Mayor: Samuel Bickerton Harman

Aldermen

St. Andrew	Geo. D'Arcy Boulton	Robt. Bell	Samuel D. Harman
St. David	Arthur Lepper	Wm. Adamson	Patrick Hynes
St. George	Thos. Smith	John Clements	John J. Vickers
St. James	James B. Boustead	Alex. Henderson	Joseph Sheard
St. John	Francis Riddell	Jas. E. Smith	John Boxall
St. Lawrence	Francis H. Medcalf	Alex. Manning	Wm. Strachan
	Wm. Hamilton, Jr.		
St. Patrick	Nathaniel Dickey	John Baxter	Robt. A. Harrison

Mr. Medcalf resigned on November 1st and Mr. Hamilton filled out the year.

1870

Mayor: Samuel Bickerton Harman

Aldermen

St. Andrew	Samuel B. Harman	Geo. D'Arcy Boulton	Robt. Bell
St. David	Patrick Hynes	Arthur Lepper	Wm. Adamson
St. George	John J. Vickers	Thos. Smith	John Clements
St. James	Jospeh Sheard	James B. Boustead	Alex. Henderson
St. John	Francis H. Medcalf	Francis Riddell	James E. Smith
St. Lawrence	Alex. Manning	Wm. Hamilton, Jr.	Wm. Strachan
			John Hallam
St. Patrick	John Canavan	Nathaniel Dickey	John Baxter

Mr. Strachan was unseated and Mr. Hallam succeeded him.

149

Mayor: Joseph Sheard

Aldermen

St. Andrew	Samuel B. Harman	Wm. Moulds	Joseph Howson
St. David	Patrick Hynes	Wm. Adamson	James J. Vance
			Arch. A. Riddell
St. George	Thos. Dick	Lewis Moffatt	John Turner
St. James	Joseph Sheard	James B. Boustead	Alex. Henderson
St. John	Francis H. Medcalf	Francis Riddell	Warring Kennedy
St. Lawrence	Alex. Manning	Wm. Hamilton, Jr.	John Hallam
St. Patrick	John Baxter	Nathaniel Dickey	John Canavan

1872

Mayor: Joseph Sheard

Aldermen

St. Andrew	Samuel B. Harman	Henry Godson	Robt. Bell
	John Carr		
St. David	Patrick Hynes	Wm. Adamson	Emerson Coatsworth
St. George	Lewis Moffatt	Thos. Dick	John Turner
St. James	Joseph Sheard	James B. Boustead	Alex. Henderson
		Wm. Hewitt	
St. John	Francis Riddell	Wm. Thompson	John Bugg
St. Lawrence	Alex. Manning	Wm. Hamilton, Jr.	John Hallam
St. Patrick	John Canavan	John Baxter	John Kerr

1873

Mayor: Alexander Manning

Aldermen

St. Andrew	John Carr	Robert Bell	Wm. Thomas
St. David	Thos. Davies	J.J. Withrow	Wm. Adamson
St. George	John Turner	John Clements	Wm. Thomson
St. James	Joseph Sheard	Alex. Henderson	John Morison
St. John	Thos. Downey	James Spence	Fred W. Coate
St. Lawrence	Alex. Manning	Wm. Hamilton, Jr.	Patrick G. Close
St. Patrick	John Mallon	John Ball	H.L. Hime

1874

Mayor: Francis H. Medcalf

Aldermen

St. Andrew	James R. Dunn	Wm. W. Farley	Daniel Hayes
St. David	Thos. Davies	John Blevins	James Martin
St. George	John Clements	W.W. Colwell	Rich. Tinning
St. James	Joseph Sheard	Alex. Henderson	James B. Boustead
St. John	Thos. Downey	James Spence	Joseph Gearing
St. Lawrence	Patrick G. Close	James Britton	Wm. Hamilton, Jr.
St. Patrick	John Ball	John Baxter	John Mallon
St. Thomas	Wm. Adamson	John J. Withrow	S.S. Mutton

Mayor: Francis H. Medcalf

Aldermen

St. Andrew	Wm. W. Farley	Daniel Hayes	James R. Dunn
			John Cornell
St. David	Wm. Adamson	James Martin	John Blevins
St. George	John Turner	W.W. Colwell	Richard Tinning
St. James	Joseph Sheard	Alex. Henderson	James B. Boustead
St. John	Thos. Downey	Jos. Gearing	James Spence
St. Lawrence	Wm. Hamilton, Jr.	Patrick G. Close	James Britton
St. Patrick	John Baxter	John Ball	James Crocker
St. Thomas	John J. Withrow	John Ritchie	S.S. Mutton

1876

Mayor: Angus Morrison

Aldermen

St. Andrew	John Cornell	Wm. W. Farley	Wm. Burke
			Francis Riddell
St. David	John Blevins	Thos. Davies	Wm. Adamson
St. George	John Turner	Wm. W. Colwell	Richard Tinning
St. James	Joseph Sheard	James B. Boustead	Alex. Henderson
St. John	Joseph Gearing	Wm. Stanley	Thos. Downey
St. Lawrence	John Taylor	Patrick G. Close	John Hallam
St. Patrick	Jacob P. Wagner	Joseph Wright	John Dill
St. Stephen	James Crocker	Richard L. Denison	Frederick W. Unitt
St. Thomas	John J. Withrow	Morgan Baldwin	Joseph Davids

1877

Mayor: Angus Morrison

Aldermen

St. Andrew	John Cornell	Wm. Burke	Francis Riddell
St. David	Thomas Allen	John Blevins	Wm. Adamson
St. George	Patrick Hughes	Arthur R. Boswell	W.W. Colwell
St. James	James Beatty, Jr.	Alex. McGregor	John Smith
St. John	Harry Piper	R. Irving Walker	James McGee
St. Lawrence	John Hallam	Patrick G. Close	John Small
St. Patrick	Joseph Wright	John Dill	John Ball
St. Stephen	James Crocker	Frederick W. Unitt	John Canavan
St. Thomas	John J. Withrow	John Ritchie	Morgan Baldwin

1878

Mayor: Angus Morrison

Aldermen

St. Andrew	Wm. W. Farley	John Cornell	Francis Riddell
St. David	John Blevins	Wm. Adamson	Thos. Allen
St. George	Patrick Hughes	John Turner	Arthur R. Boswell
St. James	John Smith	Alex. McGregor	James B. Boustead

St. John	Geo. L. Tizard	Harry Piper	James McGee
St. Lawrence	Patrick G. Close	John Hallam	John Small
St. Patrick	John Dill	John Ball	James Skyes
St. Stephen	James Crocker	Richard L. Denison	John Winchester
St. Thomas	John J. Withrow	Morgan Baldwin	John Ritchie

1879

Mayor: James Beaty, Jr.

Aldermen

St. Andrew	Wm. Dixon	Samuel Wilson	Wm. W. Farley
St. David	Thos. Allen	John Blevins	Wm. Adamson
St. George	Henry E. Clarke	Arthur P. Boswell	Peter Ryan
St. James	Neil C. Love	John Smith	W.B. Scarth
St. John	Harry Piper	James Fleming	Henry E. Hamilton
St. Lawrence	John Hallam	Robt. B. Hamilton	John Small
St. Patrick	Wm. B. McMurrich	Geo. M. Evans	John Baxter
St. Stephen	James Crocker	John Winchester	Fred. C. Denison
St. Thomas	Morgan Baldwin	Joseph Davids	Wm. Carlyle

1880

Mayor: James Beaty, Jr.

Aldermen

St. Andrew	John E. Mitchell	James H. Morris	W.W. Farley
St. David	John Blevins	James Lobb	Wm. Adamson
St. George	Peter Ryan	David Walker	H.W. Darling
St. James	N.L. Steiner	Neil C. Love	R.H. Oates
St. John	John Irwin	James Fleming	Harry L. Piper
St. Patrick	Wm. B. McMurrich	Geo. M. Evans	John Baxter
St. Lawrence	John Hallam	John Taylor	Patrick G. Close
St. Stephen	James Crocker	Fred. C. Denison	Jas. S. McMurray
St. Thomas	Wm. Carlyle	Samuel Trees	Morgan Baldwin

1881

Mayor: William Barclay McMurrich

Aldermen

St. Andrew	H.E. Clarke	John E. Mitchell	Wm. W. Farley
St. David	John Blevins	Wm. Adamson	Jas. Lobb
St. George	Arthur R. Boswell	Peter Ryan	David Walker
St. James	Neil C. Love	Newman L. Steiner	James B. Boustead
St. John	John Kent	James Irwin	James Fleming
St. Lawrence	Thos. Davies	John Hallam	John Taylor
St. Patrick	John Ball	Geo. M. Evans	John Baxter
St. Stephen	James Crocker	Fred. C. Denison	Wm. Bell
St. Thomas	Wm. Carlyle	Samuel Trees	John N. Lake

1882

Mayor: William Barclay McMurrich

152

Aldermen

St. Andrew	Henry E. Clarke	Wm. W. Farley	Daniel M. Defoe
St. George	John Maughan	Arthur R. Boswell	Peter Ryan
St. John	John Irwin	Thos. Downey	John Kent
St. Patrick	Geo. M. Evans	John Turner	John Low
St. David	George Booth	John Blevins	Wm. Adamson
St. James	Neil C. Love	W.B. Scarth	James B. Boustead
St. Lawrence	Thos. Davies	John Taylor	John Hallam
St. Stephen	Wm. Bell	Geo. Evans	John Woods
St. Thomas	Wm. Carlyle	Wm. Sheppard	Samuel Trees

1883

Mayor: Arthur Radcliffe Boswell

Aldermen

St. Andrew	Henry E. Clarke	Wm. W. Farley	Wm. Hall
St. George	David Walker	John Maughan	Peter Ryan
St. John	Thos. Downey	Harry L. Piper	John Irwin
St. Patrick	John Turner	Geo. M. Evans	John Baxter
St. Stephen	Wm. Bell	Geo. Evans	Fred. C. Denison
	Jas. Crocker	Thos. Murray	
St. David	Wm. Adamson	Geo. Booth	John Blevins
		Thos. Allen	
St. James	Newman L. Steiner	Neil C. Love	Wallace Millichamp
St. Lawrence	Thos. Davies	James Pape	John Hallam
			Geo. Leslie, Jr.
St. Thomas	Wm. Carlyle	Wm. Sheppard	Samuel Trees
St. Paul	Bernard Saunders	John T. Moore	Thos. A. Hastings

Resignations were received during the year from Geo. Booth, John Hallam, Wm. Bell, and Geo. Evans.

1884

Mayor: Arthur Radcliffe Boswell

Aldermen

St. Andrew	Wm. W. Farley	John E. Mitchell	Daniel M. Defoe
St. David	John Blevins	Thos. Allen	Wm. Adamson
St. George	John Maughan	Geo. Verral	David Walker
St. James	Neil C. Love	Newman L. Steiner	Wallace Millichamp
St. Mark	John McConnell, M.D.	C.L. Denison	M.J. Woods
St. Matthew	John Jones	J.A. Carrol	Thos. W. Elliott
St. Patrick	John Harvie	Jas. Brandon	John Turner
St. Paul	Thos. A. Hastings	John T. Moore	John Shaw
St. Stephen	James Crocker	Fred. C. Denison	Ed. W. Barton
		Septimus A. Denison	
St. Lawrence	James Lobb	James Pape	Thos. Davies
St. Thomas	Geo. B. Smith	Wm. Carlyle	Wm. Sheppard

Col. Fred. C. Denison resigned to take command of the Canadian Voyageurs who were despatched to aid in the Nile campaign for the relief of General Gordon at Khartoum.

Mayor: Alexander Manning

Aldermen

St. Andrew	Daniel M. Defoe	Wm. Hall	John E. Mitchell
St. David	Daniel Lamb	Thos. Allen	Wm. Adamson
St. George	David Walker	Geo. Verral	John Maughan
St. James	Newman L. Steiner	James Gormley	John McMillan
St. John	Thos. Hunter	Harry L. Piper	John Irwin
St. Lawrence	Thos. Taylor	Garrett F. Frankland	John James
St. Mark	Michael J. Woods	John Woods	Wm. J. McKenzie
St. Matthew	John Jones	Thos. W. Elliott	Wm. J. Smith
St. Patrick	James Brandon	John Baxter	James Pepler
St. Paul	Thos. A. Hastings	Bernard Saunders	John Shaw
St. Stephen	Edward W. Barton	Septimus A. Denison	Follis Johnston
		James Crocker	
St. Thomas	Wm. Carlyle	Edward Galley	Wm. Sheppard

Ald. Septimus Denison resigned in September to rejoin his regiment in England.

1886

Mayor: William Holmes Howland

Aldermen

St. Andrew	Daniel M. Defoe	Wm. Carlyle	Wm. Hall
St. Mark	Michael J. Woods	John Woods	Chas. L. Denison
St. David	Daniel Lamb	Robt.J. Fleming	Thos. Allen
St. Matthew	John Jones	Ernest A. Macdonald	Thos. W. Elliott
St. George	David Walker	John Maughan	Geo. Verral
St. Patrick	James Pepler	John Baxter	John Low
St. James	Newman L. Steiner	John McMillan	James B. Boustead
St. Paul	Thos. A. Hastings	Bernard Saunders	John Shaw
	Wm. Roaf		
St. John	Thos. Hunter	Harry L. Piper	John Irwin
St. Stephen	James Crocker	Edward W. Barton	Follis Johnston
St. Lawrence	John James	Garrett F. Frankland	John Turner
St. Thomas	Wm. Carlyle	Edward Galley	Philip H. Drayton

1887

Mayor: William Holmes Howland

Aldermen

St. Andrew	Daniel M. Defoe	Wm. Carlyle	E. King Dodds
St. Mark	Michael J. Woods	John Ritchie, Jr.	Chas. L. Denison
St. David	Robt. J. Fleming	Samuel R. Wickett	John C. Swait
St. Matthew	John Jones	Ernest A. Macdonald	Joshua Ingham
St. George	John Maughan	Geo. Verral	Geo. E. Gillespie
St. Patrick	John Harvie	Geo. J. St. Leger	John Baxter
St. James	James B. Boustead	John McMillan	Wallace Millichamp
St. Paul	Wm. J. Hill	John Shaw	Wm. Roaf
St. John	Harry L. Piper	Thos. Hunter	John Irwin

St. Stephen	Edward W. Barton	Follis Johnston	Robt. H. Graham
St. Lawrence	James L. Morrison	Elias Rogers	G.F. Frankland
St. Thomas	Wm. Carlyle	Edward Galley	Philip H. Drayton

1888

Mayor: Edward Frederick Clarke

Aldermen

St. Andrew	E. King Dodds	Wm. Carlyle	Thos. Pells
St. Mark	John Ritchie, Jr.	Chas. L. Denison	Michael J. Woods
St. David	John C. Swait	Wm. H. Gibbs	Robt. J. Fleming
St. Matthew	John Jones	Francis E. Galbraith	Peter Macdonald
St. George	John Maughan	Geo. Verral	Geo. E. Gillespie
St. Patrick	John Baxter	John Harvie	Geo. J. St. Leger
St. James	Alfred McDougall	John McMillan	James B. Boustead
St. Paul	Wm. J. Hill	John Shaw	Wm. Roaf
St. John	Harry L. Piper	John Irwin	Abel H. Gilbert
St. Stephen	Follis Johnston	Wm. Bell	Edward W. Barton
St. Lawrence	G.F. Frankland	John Hallam	James L. Morrison
St. Thomas	Wm. Carlyle	Edward Hewitt	Philip H. Drayton

Alderman Jones resigned in October and was named Street Commissioner.

1889

Mayor: Edward Frederick Clarke

Aldermen

St. Andrew	E. King Dodds	John E. Verral	Wm. Carlyle
St. Mark	Chas. L. Denison	Michael J. Woods	John Ritchie, Jr.
St. David	Robt. J. Fleming	Wm. H. Gibbs	John C. Swait
St. Matthew	Ernest A. Macdonald	Francis E. Galbraith	Peter Macdonald
		Geo. S. Macdonald	
St. George	Geo. E. Gillespie	John Maughan	George Verral
St. Patrick	John Baxter	Miles Vokes	Geo. J. St. Leger
St. James	Alfred McDougall	John McMillan	James B. Boustead
St. Paul	John Shaw	Wm. Roaf	Wm. J. Hill
St. John	Joseph Tait	Frank Moses	A.H. Gilbert
St. Stephen	Wm. Bell	James Crocker	Robt. H. Graham
St. Lawrence	Chas. E. Small	Thos. Davies	G.F. Frankland
St. Thomas	Wm. Carlyle	Edward Hewitt	Thos. McMullen
St. Alban	Geo. S. Booth	James Gowanlock	Isaac Lennox

1890

Mayor: Edward Frederick Clarke

Aldermen

St. Alban	Geo. S. Booth	James Gowanlock	Isaac Lennox
St. Andrew	Wm. Carlyle	E. King Dodds	John E. Verral
St. David	Wm. H. Gibbs	John C. Swait	Thos. Allen
St. George	Geo. Verral	Geo. E. Gillespie	John Maughan
St. James	James B. Boustead	Alfred McDougall	E.A. Macdonald

155

St. John	Frank Moses	Richard J. Score	John Irwin
St. Lawrence	John Hallam	Chas. C. Small	G.F. Frankland
St. Mark	John Ritchie, Jr.	Geo. G.S. Lindsey	Chas. L. Denison
St. Matthew	John Knox Leslie	Geo. S. Macdonald	Peter Macdonald
St. Patrick	John Baxter	Miles Vokes	John Lucas
	James Brandon		
St. Paul	Wm. J. Hill	Bernard Saunders	John Shaw
St. Stephen	Wm. Bell	Robt. H. Graham	John Bailey
St. Thomas	Wm. Carlyle	Edward Hewitt	Thos. McMullen

Alderman Baxter resigned in January.

1891

Mayor: Edward Frederick Clarke

Aldermen

St. Alban	Hugh McMath	Wm. P. Atkinson	James Gowanlock
St. Andrew	Wm. Burns	John E. Verral	James Kerr
St. David	Wm. H. Gibbs	Thos. Allen	Thos. Foster
St. George	Geo. E. Gillespie	Geo. McMurrich	Geo. Verral
	John Flett		
St. James	Alfred McDougall	Wm. M. Hall	James B. Boustead
St. John	Geo. M. Rose	Richard J. Score	Robt. J. Stanley
St. Lawrence	Chas. C. Small	John Hallam	James Pape
St. Mark	Geo. G.S. Lindsey	J. Orlando Orr, M.D.	John Maloney
	Wm. Crealock		
St. Matthew	Peter Macdonald	John K. Leslie	Wm. T. Stewart
St. Patrick	James Jolliffe	John Lucas	Fred. W. Phillips
St. Paul	Bernard Saunders	Wm. J. Hill	John Shaw
St. Stephen	Wm. Bell	John Bailey	Robt. H. Graham
St. Thomas	Edward Hewitt	Wm. W. Park	Ewart Farquhar

Mr. Gillespie died in April, and Mr. Lindsey resigned in September.

1892

Mayor: Robert John Fleming

Aldermen

Ward 1	Chas. C. Small	John K. Leslie	Geo. S. Macdonald	Wm. T. Stewart
Ward 2	John Hallam	Daniel Lamb	Thomas Foster	David Carlyle
Ward 3	Bernard Saunders	Richard J. Score	Geo. McMurrich	John Shaw
Ward 4	Wm. Carlyle	Wm. Burns	James Jolliffe	George Verral
Ward 5	Wm. Bell	Thos. Crawford	Robt. H. Graham	John Bailey
Ward 6	James Gowanlock	Wm. P. Atkinson	J.O. Orr, M.D.	John Maloney

In this year the Wards were re-arranged and numbered.

1893

Mayor: Robert John Fleming

Aldermen

Ward 1	Wm. T. Stewart	Chas. C. Small	Thos. Davies	John K. Leslie
Ward 2	Daniel Lamb	John Hallam	G.F. Frankland	Edward Hewitt
Ward 3	Bernard Saunders	Geo. McMurrich	John Shaw	William J. Hill
Ward 4	Wm. Carlyle	Wm. Burns	James Jolliffe	Geo. Verral
Ward 5	Wm. Bell	Thos. Crawford	John Bailey	John E. Verral
Ward 6	J.O. Orr, M.D.	Adam Lynd, M.D.	Thos. Murray	John Maloney

1894

Mayor: Warring Kennedy

Aldermen

Ward 1	Wm. T. Stewart	Thos. Allen	H.R. Frankland	Peter Macdonald
Ward 2	John Hallam	Daniel Lamb	Edward Hewitt	Thos. Foster
Ward 3	John Shaw	Geo. McMurrich	J. Enoch Thompson	Oliver B. Sheppard
Ward 4	Wm. Burns	Wm. P. Hubbard	James Jolliffe	James Crane
Ward 5	Thos. Crawford	John Bailey	John Dunn	Andrew Bates
Ward 6	Wm. P. Atkinson	John J. Graham	Thos. Murray	James Gowanlock

1895

Mayor: Warring Kennedy

Aldermen

Ward 1	Thos. Allen	Edward Blong	John K. Leslie	H.R. Frankland
Ward 2	Daniel Lamb	John Hallam	Joseph Oliver	Thos. Davies
Ward 3	Geo. McMurrich	John Shaw	Bernard Saunders	O.B. Sheppard
Ward 4	Wm. Burns	Wm. P. Hubbard	James Crane	James Jolliffe
Ward 5	Robt. H. Graham	John Dunn	Wm. Bell	Andrew Bates
Ward 6	James Scott	Thos. Murray	James Gowanlock	G.G. Rowe, M.D.
	John J. Graham			

Mr. Murray died in May and was succeeded by Mr. Gowanlock.

1896

Mayor: Robert John Fleming

Aldermen

Ward 1	Thos. Allen	John K. Leslie	Chas. C. Small	E.A. Macdonald
				John Russell
Ward 2	Francis S. Spence	John Hallam	Thos. Davies	Daniel Lamb
Ward 3	O.B. Sheppard	Bernard Saunders	Geo. McMurrich	J.B. Boustead
Ward 4	Wm. Burns	Wm. P. Hubbard	James Crane	James Jolliffe
Ward 5	Wm. Bell	Wm. T.R. Preston	Robt. H. Graham	John Dunn
Ward 6	James Gowanlock	James Scott	John J. Graham	G.G. Rowe, M.D.

Mr. Macdonald was unseated by judicial decision and was succeeded by Mr. Russell in April.

1897

Mayor: Robert John Fleming (until Aug. 5th)
John Shaw

Aldermen

Ward 1	John Russell	Thos. Allen	John K. Leslie	James Frame
Ward 2	John Hallam	Francis S. Spence	Daniel Lamb	Wm. L. Beale
Ward 3	A.F. Rutter	John Shaw	O.B. Sheppard	Bernard Saunders
Ward 4	Wm. P. Hubbard	Wm. Burns	James Crane	Wm. Carlyle
Ward 5	Robt. H. Graham	Wm. T.R. Preston	Francis H. Woods	John Dunn
Ward 6	James Gowanlock	James Scott	John J. Graham	Adam Lynd, M.D.

1898

Mayor: John Shaw

Aldermen

Ward 1	F.H. Richardson	James Frame	H.R. Frankland	J.K. Leslie
Ward 2	Thos. Bryce	Daniel Lamb	Thos. Davies	John Hallam
Ward 3	Geo. McMurrich	Bernard Saunders	O.B. Sheppard	R.J. Score
Ward 4	Wm. Burns	Wm. P. Hubbard	James Crane	Edward Hanlan
Ward 5	Francis H. Woods	John Dunn	Robt. H. Graham	A.R. Denison
Ward 6	John M. Bowman	James Gowanlock	Adam Lynd, M.D.	John J. Graham

1899

Mayor: John Shaw

Aldermen

Ward 1	James Frame	John Russell	H.R. Frankland	Wm. T. Stewart
Ward 2	John Hallam	Daniel Lamb	Francis S. Spence	Thos. Davies
Ward 3	O.B. Sheppard	Bernard Saunders	R.J. Score	N.L. Steiner
Ward 4	Wm. Burns	James Crane	Edward Hanlan	Wm. P. Hubbard
Ward 5	A.R. Denison	Francis H. Woods	John Dunn	Robt. H. Graham
Ward 6	John J. Graham	James Gowanlock	James M. Bowman	Adam Lynd, M.D.